iPhone
The Handy Guide

Matthew Stone

Thank you for downloading this book!

In order to thank you, **I would like to offer you a complementary download** about 5 social media marketing tips you should know before reading this book.

CLICK HERE TO GET IT AND STAY IN TOUCH

financial, medical or professional advice. The content of this book has been derived from various sources. Please consult a licensed professional before attempting any techniques outlined in this book.

By reading this document, the reader agrees that under no circumstances are is the author responsible for any losses, direct or indirect, which are incurred as a result of the use of information contained within this document, including, but not limited to, —errors, omissions, or inaccuracies.

Table of Contents

BOOK 1
THE HANDY GUIDE
FOR YOUR IPHONE X

Introduction

The iPhone X is more than just an iPhone; it is a significant device in the history of iPhones and Apple as a brand. Over the years, smartphones have been upgraded in terms of size and other key features that the modern user is excited about. However, Apple has remained coy about going in the same direction with their devices.

Released alongside the iPhone X are the iPhone 8 and iPhone 8 Plus. These are amazing devices. However, there is not much innovation in them as there is in the iPhone X, which seems to hold them back from the kind of appeal that they should command in the market. In terms of the design, the iPhone X powers through, ushering in a new era.

The demand for the iPhone X has been incredible, given that it was the most advanced of the three devices. What sets the iPhone X apart from most of the devices that Apple has released over the years is the intuitiveness in the features. This is a device that was built to signal a new era to give users and enthusiasts an idea of what Apple has in store for years to come.

For many people, the iPhone X is bringing

in changes that would need some time getting used to. We will share with you some useful tips and tricks that should make your work more comfortable when using the iPhone X.

iPhone X is about bringing the future to iPhone users today. The gorgeous device features a 5.8-inch Super Retina display, improved rear camera, and dual optical image stabilization. iPhone X was released and made available in more than 50 countries all over the world.

Jony Ive, the chief design officer at Apple, mentioned during the launch that Apple had been working on coming up with an iPhone that is focused on display for more than a decade. The concept behind the iPhone X and subsequent phones that will be released in the future is to offer users a balanced tradeoff between physical appearance and feel of the device and user experience.

There are a lot of remarkable new technologies that are built into the iPhone

X, technologies that will be the framework upon which Apple builds phones for the future. The all-screen display is a stunning revolutionary design and coupled with one of the most durable glass screens in the smartphone world, and the iPhone X is one device that most people will be dying to get their hands on.

Chapter 1: iPhone X Design

What Apple did with the design of the iPhone X is to fuse the old and the new to produce a fantastic phone that can compete favorably in a market dominated by dynamic shifts in consumer preferences. The bezel on the iPhone X has been cut back, and it gets a glass back.

Users who are familiar with Apple devices will appreciate the familiarity in the shape of the device. You get the same feeling with the iPhone X on your hand like you did with the iPhone 3G from back in the day. Apple has still managed to keep the premium feel to their devices. When you hold the device in your hands, you can feel it is an expensive device. The impressively curved glass blends in well with the steel rim.

For all the good that comes with the iPhone X, perhaps what you need to be careful about is how you handle it. The outer surface attracts dirt and fingerprints, as does the glass front and the back cover. You will want to make sure your hands are clean when using your iPhone X.

Another feature that Apple considered in their design is making a phone that you can use with one hand without worrying about anything. You can balance it well in one hand, and the metal-and-glass build further makes this relatively easier with reasonable grip.

The speakers are built into the iPhone X expertly, delivering impressive sound quality. If you blast the phone at full volume, it should reverberate with amazing sound quality. One of the speakers on the iPhone X faces downward, though this should not stop you from having a good experience. Even without headphones, you can still watch movies and music videos. The sound is so powerful, and you can listen to your media playing in an office full of colleagues.

The iPhone X is a durable phone and maintains the dust- and water-resistance settings. iPhone X is rated IP67 for water and dust resistance. These, however, are not permanent conditions. Over time and through wear and tear, the resistance might reduce. It is advisable that even if your phone survives a water experience, you should never charge it when it is still wet. It is only available in 64 GB and 256 GB, though the price might vary depending on the seller you are getting yours from.

Are you looking forward to enjoying your music with your earphones? Well, Apple did away with the headphone jack in an attempt to convince users that perhaps it is time to stop using 3.5 mm headphones and, in their place, introduce Airpods. Once again, the issue of Apple capitalizing on accessories comes into play. Users who do not have a perfect pair of Bluetooth headphones will struggle to appreciate this change or if perhaps you lose the adapter that comes packed in the iPhone X box.

Apple built an OLED screen, dubbed the Super Retina display into the iPhone X. It comes with a True Tone 2436×1125-pixel resolution, which at 458 ppi delivers a 1,000,000:1 contrast ratio. This sets it apart from the iPhone 8, whose display only offers 1334×750-pixel resolution at 326 ppi and a contrast ratio of 1400:1.

The colors on the iPhone X are amazing. They are bright and bold, bringing more life to the true whites, while the black shades are absolute. Compared to the iPhone 8 Plus, the yellow shades on the iPhone X are impressive, too, delivering a lively user experience regarding colors.

The iPhone X display also has an HDR (high

dynamic range) feature that expands the color and contrast range. When watching a movie or music video that has a lot of dark scenes on the iPhone X, you can watch the scenes with more clarity than you would watch on any of the older iPhone devices.

Chapter 2: iPhone X Processor

Apple introduced the iPhone X powered by an A11 Bionic SoC (system on a chip) processor. This chip is built with two high-performance cores, making it faster and 25% more efficient than the predecessor, Apple A10. The A11 bionic processor also has four high-efficiency cores, making it perform at a 70% faster rate than the high-efficiency cores that come with the A10.

One of the features that stand out about the A10 bionic processor is the fact that it runs dedicated neural network hardware, which Apple has dubbed a Neural Engine. The neural engine is built to perform up to 600 billion operations a second. This is the power that supports the amazing features built into the iPhone X, such as machine learning, Animoji, and Face ID.

Without the neural engine, Apple would have had to use the GPU or the CPU to perform tasks, yet this would be energy-intensive. The neural engine, therefore, allows iPhone X users to enjoy the benefits of machine learning and implementing a neural network efficiently.

Apple has stayed ahead of the pack by building the CPU cores for their devices over the years to a point where they compete against themselves. While most of the competition in the likes of Qualcomm and Samsung strive to work with single-threaded performance, Apple focuses on higher counts. This gives the Apple devices like the iPhone X a high-performance dual-core architecture without being energy- and resource-intensive.

The A11 bionic processor has six CPU cores, but only two of these cores are high-performance chips. The rest of the cores are high power cores. Concerning performance, the A11 bionic is faster than an iPad Pro and performs 22% faster than an iPhone 7. According to experts, the A11 bionic performs better than an Intel Core i5-7267U that powers the 13-inch Apple MacBook Pro.

Chapter 3: iPhone X Battery

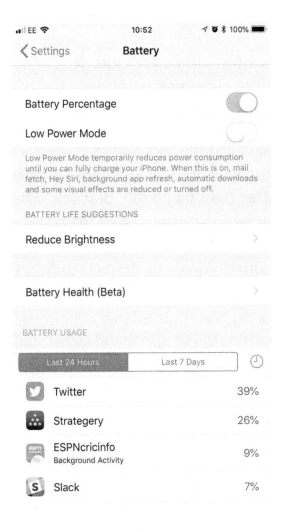

Apple built a 2716 mAh battery into the iPhone X. With this battery, users can get through a day without worrying about losing charge. There was speculation about the battery when Apple released the iPhone X with expectations that the iPhone X battery would only offer two more hours than the iPhone 7. However, practically the iPhone X performs much better than that.

Die-hard Apple fans can now look forward to using a device whose battery does not run out after barely one day of work, which has been a bother with most of the older iPhone models. Alongside iPhone 8 and iPhone 8 Plus, the iPhone X is one of the first iPhone devices that support wireless charging. Of course, at the time this was being released, Android users were already enjoying wireless charging, but for iPhone users, this is a welcome advancement.

The iPhone X uses the Qi charging standard, the same protocol that is used in the Samsung Galaxy S9. The beauty of this is that you can power your iPhone through a variety of pads, instead of being limited to a charging pad that is built by and for Apple devices.

Apple has since released their AirPower pads, though users can still power their iPhone X devices with a Mophie pad or a Belkin. Sadly, Apple does not ship the iPhone X with a fast-charge device. This is one of the concerns that many users have raised about Apple in the past, capitalizing on the sale of accessories. For the price at which the iPhone X is sold, it should at least come with all the necessary accessories.

Without the fast-charge device, however, you can still get a MacBook USB-C plug an iPad charger or a USB-C to Lightning cable. Compared to some of the devices that are available in the market, the battery life on the iPhone X is not exactly mind-blowing but still good enough to deliver a good performance all around.

One of the best things about the iPhone X battery is the way you can power through it and watch a movie even with 5% battery life left, especially when you turn on power-saving mode. This should give you around half an hour of movie time before the phone gives in.

On heavy use, which includes running WhatsApp, streaming on Bluetooth, browsing the internet, and using Facebook, you can get an impressive 18 hours of battery life off your iPhone X. The OLED technology is one of the reasons behind the impressive performance of this battery, given that it drains power less than the older models.

When running a movie for 90 minutes on 100% charge, the iPhone X stands out among other devices like the iPhone 8 Plus, which loses around 25% of battery life against 10% on the iPhone X. This is incredible, mainly since the iPhone X is built with more pixels.

When charging the phone, the iPhone X needs 2 hours and 15 minutes to get it fully charged from 0%, but only if you turn on airplane mode. Fifteen minutes of charging the device should give you around 20% of battery life.

The impressive battery life in the iPhone X can be attributed to the A11 bionic fusion chip. The 10 nm manufacturing process brings a lot of the features closer together, which makes the phone more efficient. The A11 bionic chip packs the perfect combination of efficiency and power on the iPhone X. Considering the size of the battery, the iPhone X is considered to be more of a phablet than a smartphone, especially when you compare the size of the battery and the size of the screen.

View Battery Percentage

By default, iOS is built in such a way that it does not show the battery percentage remaining. However, you can still turn this on in your Settings app. The iPhone X, however, comes without this setting. To see how much battery power you have on your phone, swipe down on the right side of the notch. The ability to view remaining battery power has been built into the Control Center.

Saving Battery Life

One of the things that many people appreciate about the iPhone X is how long the battery can run. Given all the things that you can do with this phone, a battery that can push you one and a half days is terrific. However, the iPhone X is capable of drawing the battery out for much longer.

According to experts, you can save up to 60% more on battery life. There are simple changes that you can make, like using grayscale mode, black wallpaper, or creating a pseudo-dark mode by inverting colors.

All these are possible because of the OLED display used on the iPhone X. You cannot do this on LCD screens, though, because their pixels are backlit across the board. OLED screens, on the other hand, have all their pixels lit individually. Therefore, by default, black pixels are not lit, they are always off, helping you conserve power.

Chapter 4: iPhone X Camera and Resolution

There are minute differences between the camera used in the iPhone X and the iPhone 8 Plus. Both of these devices come with a dual 12-megapixel sensor array. This is perfect when you need to take depth perception photos or if you need to take your photos zoomed in. On the iPhone X, you get an f/2.4 aperture compared to the f/2.8 aperture. Optical image stabilization is only present in with a wide-angle lens.

For still images, the iPhone X stands out as one of the best smartphone cameras in the market. The iPhone X is also fitted with a TrueDepth front-facing camera at 7-megapixels. This camera has some smart features that make it one of the best devices you can get your hands on, especially if you love to take selfies.

One of the reasons why you will be able to enjoy awesome portrait-mode photos is because the camera is built to sense depth when you are taking photos. Therefore, when using portrait mode, you can still use the front-facing camera and end up with some fantastic selfies.

In portrait mode, the iPhone X blurs out the background in your shots. Dive into the options and check out how to change the lighting settings for different photo scenes. Another option that you can consider with portrait mode is to crop yourself out of the background and place the photo against a black background.

Apple has added lots of options in portrait lighting, including contour light, studio light, natural light, stage light mono, and stage light. Stage mono light and stage light are useful when you need to black out the background of your photos while the rest of the options available for portrait lighting influence the way light strikes the face when taking a photo.

With the iPhone X, you can zoom up to 10 times, which allows you to take very excellent photos from far. However, most people barely worry about this, given that they can easily come closer to the subject whose photos they are taking and get a clear shot.

The rear-facing lens on the iPhone X has an

optical image stabilization feature (OIS). With OIS, you can look forward to getting impressive performance on your iPhone X even in low-light settings. This sets the iPhone X apart from other models like the iPhone 8 Plus. When you take macro photos with the iPhone X and iPhone 8 Plus, you will notice a difference, with the iPhone X photos being better, thanks to OIS.

Photos taken on the iPhone X look so amazing, especially on the OLED display. This comes down to the awesome colors and improved contrast ratio. Apple improved Live Photos in iOS 11, allowing users the ability to bounce, loop, or expose photos and share them with your friends. Overall, you have a decent camera on the iPhone X. The quality and speed of snapping photos are impressive for a flagship device, all thanks to the A11 bionic chip that powers the device.

Chapter 5: The Power of iOS 11

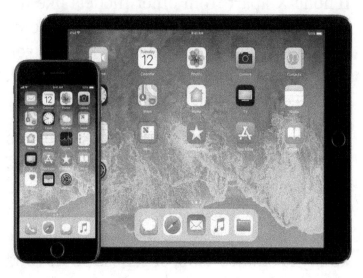

iPhone X was released running iOS 11. According to Apple CEO, Tom Cook, iOS 11 was a fusion of the most advanced and the best operating systems, delivering a powerful operating system to power a device that would be a pioneer in future iPhone developments. iOS 11 is an interactive, innovative, and amazing operating system, especially powering a device like the iPhone

X.

In design, Apple sneaked in a few subtle modifications to the interface. Texts on the iPhone X are bolder than in the predecessors. Some essential apps like Phone and Calculator have been redone and given a new look while the Control Center and the lock screen have benefitted from a complete redesign.

On the Control Center, you are free to customize it as you wish. There are lots of settings that can be modified to enhance your experience with the iPhone X. The 3D Touch integration was also expanded in iOS 11. One of the things you will notice when using your iPhone X on iOS 11 is that you no longer have to open your Settings app to alter settings.

Another feature you will love about iOS 11 is the improvements to Siri. Building on advancements in machine learning, Siri has been enhanced and is now more intelligent and with a natural voice. You can also sync your interaction with Siri on different devices so that it learns more about the way you use these devices and improve your interaction with the assistant. Other than that, Siri can now translate from English to a host of languages, like Italian, German, French, Chinese, and Spanish. Support for other languages will be added in subsequent updates.

In iOS 11, Siri gets a cross-device syncing feature. This update has transformed Siri into a faster, smarter virtual assistant. Along the same line, Apple incorporated end-to-end encryption to ensure that data sharing is only accessible by your personal devices. For example, based on this feature, Siri can recommend a topic that might interest you in Apple News, from learning your browsing habits on Safari. Siri can also remind you of an appointment that you have scheduled online.

The keyboard has also been upgraded on the iOS 11, with new features like a flick option where you can type symbols and numbers faster. At the same time, you can drag and drop items like links and images from one app into another. You can do this on your iPhone X as seamlessly as you would do it on your iPad.

Apple has introduced a Files app that works in the same way that Finder does on the MacBook, which is useful for file management, whether you have your files stored locally or on the cloud. It is compatible with third-party apps like Google Drive, One Drive, Box, and Dropbox. The Files app replaces the iCloud Drive app, and just like Finder in Mac, you can use the search function to find anything in your phone. You can also tag files with colors, set favorites, and nest folders. For developers, you can also integrate the Files app into apps that you are building, which allows you to list individual apps in the Files app.

The Settings app on iOS 11 benefits from a significant revamp. You can now add Low Power Mode to the Control Center. Other than that, you can also add your Apple TV remote to your phone, allowing you to enjoy a seamless entertainment control at home.

Chapter 6: Mastering Your iPhone X

Looking at all the devices that have been released by Apple over the years, the iPhone X stands tall among some of the most iconic models. The iPhone X was released at a time when Apple needed to advance into a new wave of telephony, embracing changes that users have wished for, especially those closely related to the experience. Android users have.

A lot of things changed in the iPhone X. The Home button, for example, went away. This did not go down well with many users, but over time, people have come to appreciate things as they are and get used to the new designs.

Apple also let go of the chunky bezel that complemented the Home button. In place of these, they gave users a screen spanning edge to edge with very slick gesture controls. The iPhone X became the basis for models that would be released later on, especially in 2018, like the iPhone XR, iPhone XS, and iPhone XS Max.

Overall, the iPhone X is an impressive phone, quite handy, and once you get used to the changes on it, especially for someone who has been using iPhones over the years, you will find it easier to use it without challenges. The following are some useful tips that will help you master your iPhone X, using it with ease, and help you get the most out of it.

Gesture Controls

One of the biggest challenges that many people have when using the iPhone X for the first time is learning to master the gesture controls. With the Home button going away, finding your way around your device can be a problem. It might feel awkward at first, but the more you get used to the device, the easier it will be for you to get accustomed to the gesture controls—you will barely miss the Home button.

To get you back to the Home grid for apps on your iPhone X, swipe from the bottom of your screen. If you want to unlock your iPhone X with Face ID, swipe up on the lock screen to access the Home functions.

Apple changed the way you can access the multitasking menu too. For this, swipe up on your phone, but do not release your finger for a brief moment. The pause on hold gesture opens the multitasking menu. From here you can navigate to any other app that is open and running. Once you have accessed the app you are interested in and want to close it, just swipe up on its image, freeing up its hold on your phone memory.

A glance down your iPhone X screen should show you a tiny bar. If you swipe right or left on that bar, you can see all the apps that are running and select the one you want. This gesture saves you time because you no longer need to open the multitasking screen to choose between a number of apps that are running.

You can change settings on your phone by accessing the Control Center. For this, swipe down from the top right corner of your screen.

Facial Recognition

Touch ID was a useful invention. It brought a different style of security into mobile devices. However, like any other tech, a few updates, and upgrades down the line, Touch ID had to go. If you were accustomed to fingerprint-level security, do not fret now that Apple has ditched Touch ID. In its place, Apple introduced Face ID.

Starting with iPhone X onward, Face ID will be rolled out in all subsequent iPhones, at least until Apple takes the game a notch higher and introduces something else in its place. Given that Face ID was being pioneered on the iPhone X, you might be excused to expect one or two glitches here and there.

However, subsequent models like the iPhone XS and iPhone XS Max have an improved Face ID, with bug fixes and patches from previous iOS updates. Therefore, if you enjoy using Face ID on your iPhone X, wait until you get your hands on the latest iPhone models—you will be amazed!

So how does Face ID work? It is simple. One steady glance at your phone, and it is unlocked. The iPhone X scans your eyes to unlock the device. Face ID is a welcome idea, given that you can also use it on Apple Pay to authorize your payments. Even when buying apps from the App Store, Face ID makes the checkout process seamless.

The struggle to remember passwords is also

a thing of the past, thanks to Face ID. Instead of having to manually key in passwords, the facial recognition program allows you to bypass entering your password.

You will get a prompt to set up Face ID when you are setting up your iPhone X for first-time use. However, if you skipped this, all is not lost. You can still finish setting it up in an instant. Go to Settings, scroll down your screen to find Face ID & Passcode, and follow the prompts to complete the registration.

One of the best things about Face ID is that once you set it up, your iPhone X will recognize you even if you put on a hat, glasses, or sunglasses. With subsequent updates, Face ID gets better at identifying your face.

Face ID Controls

Face ID is amazing. It is a genius way of controlling your device without much effort. Face ID is a welcome replacement for fingerprint access. You can create additional Face ID controls, especially when you share your device with someone.

Go to Settings, choose Face ID & Passcode, and change the settings. When you turn on Require Attention for Face ID, you have to look at your front-facing camera directly to unlock your iPhone X. This is a security feature that protects you just in case someone is trying to unlock your phone by pointing it at your face when are asleep.

Face ID Authentication Apps

Many apps have been built into the iPhone X, which use Face ID for authentication. Many other apps have since introduced this feature, especially with subsequent iOS updates. You can decide which apps you will control through Face ID, such that no one can use them without authentication. To do this, go to Settings, then Face ID & Passcode. Enter your passcode and choose Other Apps.

Unlocking Faster with Face ID

For a beginner, the easiest way to unlock your iPhone X is to raise your phone, wait for the Face ID padlock to open, and then swipe up. However, you can save time by raising and swiping on the device.

What makes it easier for you to raise and swipe at the same time is the fact that Face ID has been built so accurate that you do not need to wait that long. As long as you have the TrueDepth camera right in front of your face, you can unlock your phone faster.

Disabling Face ID

While Face ID is a welcome way of unlocking your phone, not everyone is comfortable using it. There are different situations where you might want to turn off Face ID, especially when you are at risk of someone forcing you to look at your phone to activate it.

A quick press of the power button (also identified as the side button) five times turns off Face ID by default. With Face ID turned off, the default unlock mode becomes your passcode. However, when you enter the passcode, Face ID is automatically reactivated.

Making Animojis

One of the standout features on the iPhone X is using the TrueDepth camera to make an Animoji. An Animoji allows you to convert your facial mannerisms and movements into an animated feature, like a cartoon face of an animal. It is so much fun, especially for people who love to use emojis. It gives your emojis an element of personality. The Animojis come with lots of customization options, which you can use to create an excellent cartoon version of your face and share it in your messages. Apple takes your communication and interactions on the iPhone X a notch higher with Animoji. The Animoji uses Face ID. You can record Animoji videos for 110 seconds and send them to someone on iMessage.

Managing Notifications

Notifications are awesome. They remind you of things that are happening around you. However, notifications can also be very annoying. They keep popping up at will, which might also keep you distracted from important things, especially when they pop up when you least expect them—and they always do.

Apple has introduced a workaround for this in iOS 12, where notifications from a single app are grouped together to reduce the clutter on your lock screen. On your Notification Center, swipe left on any of the notifications to reveal the Manage option. Tap on this and choose how you want to have the notifications on that app delivered to your phone.

Deliver Quietly will keep the notifications restricted to the Notification Center so they will not pop up on your screen. Alternatively, you can turn off all notifications so you can access the apps only when you choose to.

True Tone

When was the last time you had an upgrade of your iPhone? Granted, Apple devices barely ever come cheap, so most people end up taking a while before they upgrade or get a new one. If you have not had an iPhone upgrade in years, you might not have an idea what True Tone is or why it is important to you.

True Tone is a feature that automatically measures the light around you and adjusts the white level and color to match the ambient light. Why is True Tone important? Experts advise that it is a feature built to reduce eye strain and make sure that, irrespective of the lighting conditions in your environment, you can always get the right coloring on your phone.

It might take a while for you to get used to True Tone, especially if you have been accustomed to using screens that maintain the same color scheme all the time irrespective of the environmental changes around you. Your eyes, especially, will love True Tone. How can you access it? Go to Display & Brightness in your Settings app. Alternatively, you can also access True Tone through the Control Center.

Adjusting Portrait Photos

For years, portrait mode has been one of the primary features of any iPhone model. When the iPhone X was released, Apple took things a notch higher and introduced portrait mode to the front camera. The later models (iPhone XS and iPhone XS Max) have taken things further, adding depth control to portrait mode.

With depth control, you can change the focal length of your photos after the shots. This means that you can tweak the background bokeh and blur effects of your photo using the slider until you settle on the perfect setting.

Silent Alarms

An alarm goes off, and you almost get up in a rage. Blaring alarms can be quite a turnoff, and most people get irritated when a loud alarm goes off. On your iPhone X, you do not have to keep fighting with the snooze button. When your alarm goes off, pick up the phone and stare into your camera. Face ID identifies your face and automatically reduces the alarm volume.

Do Not Disturb

When you set your phone down after a long day, you need some peace and quiet. Apple created the Do Not Disturb feature to assist with this. You keep your phone silent at night, making sure that you do not have messages or notifications that abruptly interfere with your sleep.

In iOS 12, Do Not Disturb has been upgraded, with more customizable features than the default setting that comes with the iPhone X. While you can still get into Do Not Disturb mode until you turn it off, you can now set a timer on how long you want to keep your phone in Do Not Disturb mode.

Options include Do Not Disturb until morning, afternoon, evening until you exit a given location (which is perfect if you are at a specific place, like at the movies). You can also set Do Not Disturb to run alongside a calendar event so it stays on until that event is over. The Do Not Disturb icon is found in the Control Center. It looks like a crescent-shaped moon.

Activating Siri

One of the most iconic features of the iPhone has always been Siri. Siri is one amazing assistant, and over the years, advancements to the Siri tech have seen it introduced to MacBook devices and other Apple devices. The beauty of using Siri has also seen other virtual assistants come to life, like Microsoft's Cortana.

A few years down the line, Siri keeps getting better and better. On your iPhone X, you can activate Siri by pushing down your side button. The side button is available on the right-hand side of your iPhone X.

Accessing Apple Play

Apple Pay is a convenient way for you to make purchases online. It is a secure platform, and when shopping online, you can get payments done in seconds. To access Apple Pay, double tap on the side button on your iPhone X. The beauty of using Apple Pay is that you no longer have to keep looking for your credit card or debit card to pay for anything.

Using the App Switcher

Since the iPhone X does not have the Home button, most people who have been using iPhones in the past might struggle to access the App Switcher. However, Apple introduced a handy Home indicator at the bottom of the screen.

The Home indicator is helpful when you want to access the App Switcher or if you want to unlock your phone. To switch apps, press and hold the app you have opened, and drag it to the Home indicator on the right side of the screen. This gesture also reveals any of the apps that are open and lines them up in order. You can swipe right or left to access any of the running apps. You can also close any apps while swiping over them.

Accessing the Notification Center

The Notification Center gets a new name on the iPhone X, the Cover Sheet. It might take you a while to get used to this, however. To access the Cover Sheet, swipe down on your screen from the left of the notch on the top part of your iPhone.

Accessing the Control Center

To access the Control Center, use the same gesture as the Cover Sheet, but instead of left, swipe down from the right side. Instead of doing this, you can also customize your Control Center by accessing the iPhone X Settings.

Go to Settings, then Control Center, and select Customize Controls. This step will come in handy for you later on when you need to know how much battery life you have remaining on your iPhone X.

Making an Emergency Call

You can make a medical or an emergency call on your iPhone X by pressing any of the volume buttons and the side button simultaneously. The same applies if you want to turn off the iPhone X. This gesture gives you options on the screen, where you choose to make an emergency call, pull up your medical ID, or turn off your phone.

Closing Open Apps

If you have been using many apps and need to close one or all of them, you need to navigate to the App Switcher. The App Switcher is found on your Home indicator at the bottom of your iPhone X screen. Identify the app you want to close and drag it to the right side.

Press and hold onto the app you want to close briefly until a red button shows up on top of each of the app cards. Slide up on the app that you want to close. Alternatively, tap on the red button on the app to close it. This is a handy way for you to close apps that are running in the background and free up memory space and save your battery.

Taking Screenshots

Taking screenshots with your iPhone X is as simple as pressing the side button and the volume up button.

Resetting Your iPhone X

You can force a hard reset on the iPhone X if it has become unresponsive. The following three steps should get you going:

1. Press and release the volume up button.

2. Press and release the volume down button.

3. Press and hold the side button on the

right side of your phone for a few seconds until your iPhone X restarts, showing the Apple logo that appears on your screen when you turn on power.

Recording 60 fps 4K videos

With your iPhone X, you can record 4K videos, but by default, this can only happen at 30 fps. If you want a smooth and higher resolution than the default 30 fps, go to Settings, then Camera, and then select Record Video. Here you can select the ideal resolution at which you will record videos.

Tap to Wake

Tap to Wake is a function that helps you access your device screen without having to fiddle with your iPhone X too much. When you receive your iPhone X, the Tap to Wake function is set on by default. What this means is that if you tap the screen, the lock screen should appear.

While this is a good idea and it makes your

work easier when accessing the device, some people do not like it. You can turn this feature off. Go to Settings, then choose General, then Accessibility, and turn off Tap to Wake.

Zooming into YouTube

At times you need to access YouTube on full screen to enjoy a better experience of the videos you are watching. Apple introduces a feature that allows you to zoom into videos right inside the YouTube app.

Access YouTube on landscape mode then use the standard pinch-to-zoom gesture to zoom in or out of a YouTube video. When you zoom into a video, YouTube should indicate Zoomed to fill at the top of the screen until you zoom back to standard settings, upon which it will indicate Original.

Virtual Home Button

When Apple did away with the Home button, many people suffered. However, most people have done just fine without it and gotten used to the new gestures. Just in case you are finding it difficult to live without the Home button, there is a more natural way to bring it back, a virtual Home button.

Go to Settings, then General, then Accessibility, and turn on Assistive Touch. This should introduce a virtual Home button on your screen, which you can use as you please.

Once you have the virtual Home button visible, you can customize its settings and how it will respond. Choose default actions for double tap, single tap, 3D touch, or a long press. There are other settings that you can introduce into the virtual Home button, like a shortcut to launch your Control Center.

One of the beautiful things you will realize about the virtual Home button is that it is more versatile than the traditional Home button that Apple discontinued on the iPhone X. This means that you do not necessarily need to set it in the same position the traditional Home button rests. You can set your virtual Home button anywhere on the screen.

Returning Home

What happens when you are deep in your phone use, perhaps browsing or playing a game on your device, then you remember something that you should check out, prompting you to return Home? Simply swipe up from the bottom of your device.

At the bottom of the iPhone X screen, you will see a Home indicator line. This comes in handy when you are using an open app but need to access the Home screen. When you swipe from the bottom on your Home screen, the device takes you back to the first page of your open apps. This gesture is useful especially when you have a slew of app icon pages running.

Conclusion

The iPhone X is an amazing device. It is even better for someone who has had an iPhone experience over the years. If you are new to the iPhone ecosystem, you might struggle to get your way around. Avid iPhone users will, however, fall in love with the iPhone X, especially since Apple finally makes a move away from the tired design that has featured on their devices for so many years.

The iPhone X is a device that Apple produced for the users to give a glimpse of how far they are ahead of the game regarding technological advancement and to give a preview of what users can look forward to in the coming years.

On the iPhone X, Apple got a lot of things right, perhaps because they did not rush to address consumer demands over the years. The iPhone X is a phone that exudes confidence from lessons learned over the years in design and user experience. One of the best Apple devices was the iPhone 4. It ushered in a change from average specs to a device that delivered the best user experience. Since then, the iPhone X is the best device that Apple has released that offers the same experience.

It has taken Apple years to introduce an OLED screen to their devices, and it is a beautiful feature to have on the iPhone X. Users can now enjoy the same clarity that has been on flagship Android devices for years. Apple has also done an excellent job with the raw power of the selfie camera, combining it well with Face ID to deliver an all-around performance.

Going by the design, the temptation to buy the iPhone X is real. The other phones that were released alongside it, the iPhone 8 and iPhone 8 Plus still feature the traditional Apple designs that are more than four generations old, which is barely impressive at this juncture.

BOOK 2
iPhone XR
The Handy Guide

Introduction

The year 2018 was a fantastic year for iPhone lovers and enthusiasts, given the trifecta of devices that the tech giant released. Known for their high-end devices, Apple followed in the footsteps of iPhone XS and XS Max with the XR, a device dubbed as the cheapest iPhone device of the year. This sentiment alone is bound to get people excited about getting their hands on this device.

We must, however, address the fact that the term cheapest should not be misconstrued with substandard services. Even with the lowest cost offering of the iPhones released in the year, the iPhone XR still packs a punch, compared to most of the devices in the market in its price range. You still get the amazing, powerful experience you would expect from any iPhone device.

If you are buying the XR, you are looking forward to a fantastic device that has taken the smartphone market by storm – obviously! While the other devices retailed at $1,099 and $999, the XR hit the market at $749. For an average smartphone user, and we are talking Android devices here, $749 still sounds a bit pricey. For an avid iPhone user, $749 is quite a steal!

You can get the iPhone XR in the following storage capacities, and prices:

64 GB for $749

128 GB for $799

256 GB for $899

The iPhone XR runs on iOS 12. Public access to the iOS 12 was slated much earlier before the iPhone XR was, which means customers already have an experience of the new upgraded operating system. By the time you get your hands on the iPhone XR, you might expect a few updates, patches and bug fixes to the iOS already rolled out.

While the XR might look slightly different from the other iPhone devices released in the market this year, what runs under the hood is just as amazing as what you would expect from Apple. They outdid themselves on this one.

Want to have a device that stands out? iPhone XR comes in six different colors, blue, coral, yellow, red, white and black. The XS and XS Max, on the other hand, are only available in three colors each. Other than the six color options available, you can take things further, and choose to get an iPhone cover for your XR, which adds even more styling options. Regarding aesthetics, the XR is a beast.

While the XR beats the XS and XS Max on aesthetics, they beat it hands down on the camera and display features, which have been poised as their major selling points. Besides that, however, the XR, XS and XS Max are pretty much cut from the same cloth. If you are currently using an iPhone 8 or an older model, upgrading to the iPhone XR would be a brilliant idea.

Chapter 1: iPhone XR Processor

Let's start with the bionic chip. XR runs the same A12 chip that you will find in XS and XS Max. Other than the fact that it powers the higher end models of this device, what is so special about this chip? Of all the processors Apple has used over the years, the A12 bionic processor is their greatest introduction yet. The in-house system on a chip (SoC) processor combines multiple processing cores at insane energy levels, allowing you to command some intensive tasks.

For light work like browsing the internet and checking your emails, the A12 bionic processor makes quite a meal thanks to the high-efficiency cores. Six cores power this processor CPU, and an additional eight core neural engine that supports the machine learning systems built into the iPhone XR.

According to Apple, the A12 bionic chip is designed to power at least 5 trillion operations a second.

It is not easy to understand why this statistic means so much unless you compare it with the previous installment. At 7-nanometers, the A12 bionic chip processor is a breath of fresh air compared to the previous 10-nanometer A11 chip that could power through 600 billion operations a second. Given that the XR, XS and XS Max run the same A12 bionic chip, the XR is, therefore, just as compelling under the hood as the others.

Chapter 2: iPhone XR Battery at a Glance

Something you will fancy about the iPhone XR is drawing comparisons with the XS and XS Max, especially since you are paying much less to get it.

Let's have a look at the battery. The XR features a 2,942 mAh battery. Of course, this comes nowhere close to the flagship iPhones with a battery capacity of more than 4,000 mAh. However, why is this important? Well, the XS only runs a 2,658 mAh battery. So, for a few bucks less, you are getting more juice out of the XR. The XS Max, however, features a 3,174 mAh battery.

The official battery specifications for the iPhone XR according to Apple are as follows:

Up to 25 hours talk time on wireless

Up to 15 hours on internet use

Up to 16 hours video playback on wireless

Up to 65 hours audio playback on wireless

Compared to the iPhone 8 Plus, you have around one and a half hours more battery life, which makes it a good idea for someone who is looking for an upgrade.

Also, a bonus, Apple also included wireless charging on the iPhone XR.

Chapter 3: iPhone XR Display

The iPhone XR display is one of the features that has got many people talking. Many people have by now experienced the OLED screens that are popular in the market and would have expected the iPhone XR to follow suit. However, Apple decided to go with an LCD screen.

The iPhone XR, instead of going the OLED way as has been witnessed in models like iPhone X and iPhone XS, was built with LCD screens. It is an interesting decision, given that LCD screens are considered a thing of the past. However, according to Apple, the LCD used in the iPhone XR is more of a futuristic approach.

Why would Apple go this way? It is important to note that Apple still stays true to the LCD screens as their standard display technology for their devices. Even with an

LCD screen in the face of OLED competition, Apple still takes a win with the XR, given that they have designed a device that, for the very first time, has the entire front face of the camera covered. On the iPhone XR, it has been tagged the Liquid Retina display. What this means is that Apple has done away with the chin and forehead design that users have been accustomed to for a long time.

Perhaps the screen is not one of the most amazing features of the iPhone XR. While the other phones in its class come with amazing OLED displays, it only comes with an LCD screen. The 6.1 inches in your hands will perhaps make up for this if you fancy a gigantic screen. The thing with LCD screens is that they are not as bright as OLED screens. So, other than the massive screen in your hand, you should not expect the crisp, liquid clear clarity you will find in the XS and XS Max.

What makes this LCD screen different from archaic models? The screen on the iPhone

XR, like the OLED screens, is rounded from one corner to the other. It features sub-pixel and masking skills, and an additional LED back-lighting. The backlight on the iPhone XR LCD screen helps to support lightning depression and also helps to make up for the lack of 3D Touch for Haptic Touch.

Concerning screen size, the iPhone XR is, in fact, the second largest device that Apple has released. It is sandwiched in size by the iPhone XS Max and the iPhone XS. The iPhone XR comes with 6.1 inches of screen size, which is a big deal compared to 5.8 inches that we have seen in the iPhone X and iPhone XS.

If you have been looking for an upgrade in screen size, the iPhone XR will make a good candidate. It is only second to the iPhone XS Max, which comes in at 6.5 inches. For many an iPhone user, 6.1 inches is an ideal size, given that people have been asking for a long time whether Apple would follow in the footsteps of the Android competitors and release widescreen phones.

The iPhone market is advancing in light of consumer demands, and a big screen is considered something most people are looking for. There are a number of users who still appreciate the smaller devices, like the iPhone SE. However, the fact remains that people are looking forward to bigger devices, and for a good reason.

In recent years, we have seen larger phones eat into the market share for tablets, killing smaller size tablets in the process. A big screen is, considered an appropriate device that cuts across cultural and gender divides, hence the 6.1 inches on the iPhone XR is a welcome move.

We must also appreciate the fact that phones are currently one of the key communications and computing devices for most people, and the move toward a bigger screen is about increasing creativity and productivity.

Building on the screen size, the iPhone XR shares a lot of advantages with the iPhone

XS Max. One of these features is the Display Zoom, a feature that is designed to make the device more accessible. With the Display Zoom, it is easier to see things clearly on the large screen. Interactions are enhanced, and your touch capacity is also improved. This is also designed to help you navigate faster when using the iPhone XR, especially when you are going through lists with finer details.

A large screen is only as good as you can enjoy utility value from it. With the iPhone XR, you can enjoy reachability, accessing the top of your phone screen from the middle. The iPhone XR employs the X-style navigation system for gestures. It might take a while getting used to this, but when you do, you will be able to enjoy the Home button experience.

For all the good things that have been said about the iPhone XR, there is not much to look forward to about the resolution and density, unless this is your first experience with an iPhone. Those who have used iPhones over the years will notice the differences.

The iPhone XS and iPhone XS Max both feature impressive screen resolutions, at 2436 x1125 and 2688 x 1942 respectively, with 458 ppi. The iPhone XR, on the other hand, features a paltry 1792 x 828 resolution, with 326 ppi.

It might not feel right comparing an OLED screen with an LCD screen, especially when you look at the foundational design and build of the screens. They are two different technologies. When addressing the differences in terms of the advantages and disadvantages of LCD and OLED screens, the disparities are at best, relative. It would take a lot to put them side by side in a fair comparison.

A lot of people would feel an LCD screen is a step back, but this is not true. There are challenges that are faced by the OLED screens too, however advanced people believe they are. Some of the common challenges that you would experience when using an OLED screen include an off-axis color shift and black smearing. With an LCD screen, you do not have to worry about black smearing or off-axis color shift. That being said, however, LCD is simply not as alluring and desirable as an OLED screen. OLED screens offer an amazing deep black hue and a high contrast range that you would never experience in the LCD screen on the iPhone XR.

What Apple has done with the iPhone XR is to give the LCD a new lease of life, pushing it as far as they can. You can, however, not expect to get the HDR (high dynamic range) experience, but the color scheme and calibration in the iPhone XR is amazing. On this feature, the iPhone XR offers pretty much the same experience you would get in an iPhone XS.

The display on the iPhone XR is not 1080p. This does not mean you will not get an amazing experience with this device. However, unless you plan on using VR on your device where you should be getting 4K on either eye, the 326 ppi available with the iPhone XR is decent, especially for normal viewing distances.

For normal use, however, you should not notice any difference when using the iPhone XR. It is a fantastic device which promises to deliver an amazing user experience.

Chapter 4: The Power of iOS 12

One of the things you will love about the iPhone XR is iOS 12. This revamped upgrade gives you one of the best iPhone experiences to date. You are looking at an iPhone that performs faster than most, is delightful and more responsive. Everyone loves a responsive device. The iOS 12 has been dubbed one of the most advanced operating systems on mobile devices yet.

What makes it stand out?

Regarding performance, the iOS 12 is designed to help you speed things up. Everything you have been using your iPhone for in the past, you can now do the same, at insane speeds. Take swiping your camera, for example, whose response has been improved by 70%.

You are also looking at a 50% improvement

in the keyboard display speed, and if you are using your iPhone under a heavy workload, you will be able to launch apps up to two times faster than before.

The performance enhancements are some of the reasons why you are going to enjoy using the iOS 12 on your iPhone XR. Other minor enhancements go towards giving you an overall amazing experience on the iPhone XR.

Fancy some FaceTime with friends and family members? You can now interact with up to 32 people at the same time. The audio and video enhancements on the iPhone XR powered by the iOS 12 make this a lot easier. In a group setting, if someone is speaking, their tile is enlarged, allowing you to stay focused on the conversation.

iOS 12.1.1

When Apple released iOS 12.1.1, one group of users who had a lot to look forward to was iPhone XR users. With the update, you can now enjoy some of the Haptic Feedback features that were not present previously. This adds functionality to the device, especially when you use a long press to get more out of your notifications.

The updates released thus far are small, but allow you to enjoy utmost utility out of your iPhone XR. It has not been a smooth sailing experience for everyone, however. Soon after the upgrade, there have been issues with some users experiencing trouble connecting to their cellular networks. It is not a widespread concern, because the frequency of reports to this problem is random.

Other users have also reported enjoying full cellular use on their iPhone XR devices with select apps, but not all the apps. What this alludes to is that the device can identify and pick up the connection to a cellular signal, but the operating system is struggling to manage the connection.

This update includes support for third-party

navigation assistance apps instead of having to depend on Apple Maps all the time. You can look forward to using Google Maps, for example, in CarPlay for iOS 12. However, you must update to the current release. Google Maps is popular for accurate information in terms of traffic information, finding places, and alternative routes. The fact that you can enjoy it in the in-built display on your device is a plus.

Assuming that you started getting directions on your iPhone XR and then you got into your car, you simply need to connect to CarPlay and Google Maps will continue from where you left on the phone.

If you are planning your commute between your home and the workplace, Google Maps will provide you live updates on traffic so you can plan your route efficiently. You also get access to some of the favorite spots you frequent, which is a good way to remind you to pick up something you might have forgotten.

Another important feature that you will enjoy with the iOS 12.1.1 upgrade on your iPhone XR is dual SIM support. This is a feature that iPhones have barely taken seriously over the years. However, the update enables an eSIM that comes built into the iPhone XR, iPhone XS, and iPhone XS Max. Instead of getting a second physical SIM card, you can simply activate your cellular plan on a different network.

Chapter 5: iPhone XR vs iPhone XS

A lot has been said about the iPhone XR, especially when pitting it against iPhone XS. There are shared features and some dissimilarities here and there. Overall, however, these are two amazing phones. The release of the iPhone XR was marked by a lot of expectation, being that it was an exciting device, and at an affordable price.

Choosing between an iPhone and an Android device is often an easy choice because you are probably looking at the price, the brand you are loyal to, unique features, and so forth. However, if you have to choose between two or more iPhone devices, it can be quite a challenge. Price alone cannot be the deciding factor. You have to go deeper, learn more about the devices so that you make an informed decision. This comparison will pit the iPhone XR and iPhone XS.

Display

One of the first things you notice when comparing an iPhone XR and an iPhone XS is the display disparities. The iPhone XS has a smaller screen than the iPhone XR. Which one is better of the two?

Someone who fancies large screen devices will go for the iPhone XR. However, what are you getting in an iPhone XR that you cannot find in an iPhone XS, in light of the screen? Is a big screen always the better option in terms of experience and utility?

Experts contend that the iPhone XR screen is inferior to the iPhone XS. The iPhone XS has an OLED screen at 5.8 inches. The iPhone XR only has an LCD screen, at 6.1 inches.

Other than the dimensions according to size, you get True Tone 2436 x 1125 pixels at 458 ppi on the iPhone XS, compared to the

True Tone 1792 x 828 pixels at 326 ppi on the iPhone XR.

The contrast ratio on the iPhone XS is 1,000,000:1 versus 1,400:1 on the iPhone XR. The screen to body ratio is 82.9% on the iPhone XS, compared to 79.0% on the iPhone XR.

Based on the display parameters, the iPhone XR is a downgrade from OLED to LCD, compromising on a few displays comforts that most iPhone users are used to. The resolution on the iPhone XR is significantly lower. It gets so bad, and you cannot experience full HD content at 1080p on the iPhone XR. For a device that boasts of 6.1 inches of screen surface, this is a let-down. There are many devices in the market that offer far superior display parameters for a fraction of what Apple is charging for the iPhone XR.

Since the introduction of iPhone 6S, 3D Touch technology has been a prominent feature in iPhones, which is surprisingly missing in the iPhone XR. However, Apple makes up for this by making it HDR10 and Dolby Vision compliant just like the iPhone XS. This is brilliant, especially since you are able to enjoy high-quality videos on the iPhone XR.

Looking at the OLED screens, an LCD screen might not be able to pack a punch, especially when you are looking at the black levels and contrast ratio. However, for many an average iPhone user, the LCD screen is more than sufficient.

Just in case you feel the 326 ppi is not sufficient, a kind reminder would suffice, that it was the same resolution depth that was used in the iconic iPhone 8. Besides, 326 ppi is more than what you would get in a 40" 4K TV, which only serves you 110 ppi. The aspect ratio on the iPhone XR is still the same as what you get on the iPhone XS, 19:5:9. The iPhone XR also gets a True Tone color accuracy, with 120 Hz touch sensing, which allows you to enjoy a more responsive touch input.

iOS 12 brings forth a lot of advancements that make it easier for you to enjoy a variety of functions that would have been missing without 3D Touch. On the brighter side, however, there has been a slow uptake and appreciation of 3D Touch from users, and in response, Apple is shelving it altogether. In retrospect, the display is one of the biggest differences between the iPhone XR and the iPhone XS, though most people will barely care about it.

Model design and finishes

When you look at the iPhone XR and iPhone XS, the two devices almost look similar. However, they are not. There is a very small difference between the two devices:

iPhone XR - 150.9 x 75.7 x 8.3 mm (5.94 x 2.98 x 0.33 in) and 194 g (6.84 oz)

iPhone XS - 143.6 x 70.9 x 7.7 mm (5.65 x 2.79 x 0.30 in) and 177g (6.24 oz)

As you can see, the iPhone XR is slightly larger than the iPhone XR, but this also means an additional 10% in weight. This is attributed to the weight of the LCD display screen. The LCD is traditionally less flexible compared to OLED displays, which means you cannot fit it comfortably into the iPhone chassis. This explains the presence of larger bezels on the sides of the iPhone XR.

The iPhone XS gets a premium feel thanks to the stainless steel chassis, making it a fancier option than the iPhone XR. The iPhone XR features a 7000 series aluminum chassis, the same model that was used in the iPhone 8 and the predecessor models. The iPhone XR only gets an IP67 water resistance rating, compared to the IP68 water resistance rating that is used in the iPhone XS.

The IP68 rating allows you to submerge the iPhone XS in water for no more than half an hour if the water depth is no more than two meters. These are simple features that most average users would not give a care about. On the bright side, while the iPhone XR has thicker bezels compared to the iPhone XS, they still come out thinner than most of the other OLED devices that are available in the market.

Both of the devices have external stereo speakers on the left and right, which deliver 25% louder sound than their predecessors. They also have dual SIM support, and you can use an internal eSIM or a nano SIM. Therefore, you can use both your home and travel sim on the same device. The good thing about this is that it is a feature that has never been present in any iPhone device since the beginning of time.

In terms of the appeal, iPhone XS comes limited to three colors, (Gold, Space Grey, and Silver) while iPhone XR is available in six colors (Coral, Yellow, Blue, Black, White, and Red). If you are the kind of user who appreciates diversity and something that gives you true perspective, the iPhone XR is your best bet. It has even been dubbed a more interesting model of the iPhones released in 2018.

Performance

One of the things that you will appreciate about the iPhone XR is the fact that it is running the same chipset that powers the iPhone XS. These two devices are all running Apple's A12 bionic chipset. The chipset features a six-core CPU, four core GPU, and an M12 motion coprocessor.

What sets them differently that the iPhone XS is loaded with 4 GB of memory, but the iPhone XR comes in a distant second with only 3 GB. Where will you feel this difference? Most people will barely notice. However, if you are someone who likes to multitask on their device, over time, you will notice a slight lag in performance.

It might not be apparent, especially when you are running light apps. However, if you are a gamer, or you use a lot of apps that are resource intensive, you will notice a difference. The reason why your apps will lag in performance is that you have a lot of them hogging your memory space, without allowing the device to reload.

The experts at Apple do contend, however, that there is a good reason why the iPhone XS was fitted with a larger RAM than the iPhone XR. The iPhone XS has two cameras. It needs additional memory resources to power the dual camera functions. If you want to know that 3 GB on the iPhone XR is not something to frown upon, take a step back and think about the iPhone X. This device was loaded with 3 GB of RAM, but you will not come across people complaining that it is a slow device.

Demystifying the A12 Bionic Chipset

What is so special about this chipset? The term bionic attached to the name is a pure marketing gimmick. However, that should not take away the important points about this chipset. Ideally, what you are getting through this chipset is a 50% improvement in power efficiency when your iPhone XR is running idle, or in terms of the graphics performance. Other than that, you will get an improvement in the CPU performance, of up to 15% based on the predecessor model.

There is a good reason why the A12 chipset is setting Apple, and all devices that are running it, a cut above the rest. In terms of competition, iPhone X, released in 2017 is considerably faster than any other Android device that was released in 2018. This means that Apple is just that good. They do not need the power, but they are giving it to you because they can.

Whether you are getting the iPhone XR or the iPhone XS, you will appreciate the power reserve capacity in the device. How important is this to you? Power reserves help you with NFC transactions. You should be able to complete the transactions even when your battery has run out. This is a feature that Apple has built into all the devices that were released in 2018, and hopefully will be a mainstay in the future, with a few improvements, of course.

Back in the day, iPhones were built

incompatible with 600 MHz 4G bands. These bands are useful especially in areas where there was no signal. Apple has built this into the iPhone XR and the iPhone XS. This is a step in the right direction, opening up new frontiers for the tech giant.

However, even though the iPhone XR is able to support 4G, it is not fitted with the 4G Cat 16 LTE speed that is built into the iPhone XS. With this support, the iPhone XS can support downloads up to one gigabit. To be honest, this is too much power in one device. However, even without that, the iPhone XR still has a Cat 12 600 Mbit speed support, whose power is more than most average users need on their devices. There are credible reports that Apple might still be lagging behind in terms of adding 5G support to their devices. However, if you are getting such amazing speeds on your 4G enabled device, there is no reason for you to worry.

Cameras

Everything about the iPhone XR and the iPhone XS is the same when we consider optics, especially the dual rear camera. Other than the differences in display size, the only other feature that you can recognize almost immediately between these two is that the iPhone XR only has one rear camera. Let's take a closer look at the camera specifications of these two devices:

They both have a primary rear camera, 12MP, f/1.8 aperture, 1.4μm pixel size. The camera supports Optical Image stabilization (OIS), Quad-LED True Tone flash, and Portrait Lighting.

While the iPhone XR does not have a secondary rear camera, the iPhone XS has a secondary telephoto lens with the following features: 12MP, f/2.4 aperture, 1.0μm pixel size, OIS, and 2x optical zoom.

For the front camera, the two devices both have a TrueDepth camera, 7MP, f/2.2

aperture

Is it a good thing that the iPhone XR does not have 2x optical zoom on it? Some people would agree, others would be indecisive. However, how often do you need to zoom into an object to capture it? Most people just move closer to the object and take awesome shots. Bearing this in mind, you might not really miss it.

If we look at some of the earlier models, they all needed a secondary camera to help in taking good Portrait Mode shots. The iPhone XR, however, is capable of doing this with the rear and single front cameras, so you will do just fine with it.

One other thing that Apple has done on the iPhone XR and the iPhone XS is to offer HDR image processing. The beauty of HDR image processing is that you are able to combine lots of photos taken from unique exposure angles and combine them into one image. This feature was built into the devices to address an issue that Apple devices have always had since time immemorial, a weakness with dynamic range. With this in mind, the iPhone XR and iPhone XS can offer the same experience you would enjoy when you are using a Google Pixel 2, which has been dubbed one of the phones with the best cameras.

Both of the iPhones have an enlarged pixel size on the primary rear cameras. A larger pixel size makes them allow more light in, which is an important upgrade to improve photography in low light settings.

Charging and battery life

A lot of people often expect that they will get longer battery life on a more expensive device. This is not the case when you compare the iPhone XR and the iPhone XS. In terms of the battery life, we have to go back to the OLED and LCD comparison and learn something important. An LCD display does not consume as many resources as an OLED display.

The upside to using an LCD display on the iPhone XR over the OLED display used in the iPhone XS is that you are getting a low resolution on the XR than the XS. A low resolution consumes less power, and since the phone comes in a large size, Apple has enough room to load the device with a larger battery.

On the iPhone XR, you are getting 2,942 mAh, while the iPhone XS only offers 2,658 mAh. Why is this important? The iPhone XR, running this battery, is capable of lasting 25% longer than the iPhone XS on most functions. In fact, the iPhone XR can even outlast the iPhone XS Max, yet this was the flagship model.

However, there is a catch when it comes to the iPhone XR. It does not support fast wireless charging. Whether or not users will struggle to accept this, we will probably see in the next rollout of iPhone devices.

For wired charging, both the iPhone XR and iPhone XS are supported. If your device is flat out, you can get it up to 50% charging in half an hour. However, in traditional fashion, Apple still refuses to include a fast charger in the box when you buy the phone. You have to fork out an additional $75 to get the compatible cable and fast charger.

Cost consideration

If you need a wired fast charger for your devices, you will need to consider adding another $75 to your purchase price. However, that aside, the iPhone XR is still popular as the most affordable Apple device in its range.

This is how the devices compare:

iPhone XS

64GB at $999

256GB at $1,149

512GB at $1,349

iPhone XR

64GB at $749

128GB at $799

256GB at $899

Chapter 6: iPhone XR Out of the Box

Apple has bundled quite a few things inside the box. Here's a list of things you can expect to take out of the box.

IPhone XR

This is what you paid your money for. So make sure that you do not lose it.

Lightning to USB Cable

Apple is still using the charging connector it introduced with the iPhone 5 which launched in 2012. Although other members of the family have switched to the conveniently smaller USB-C connector, the iPhone XR still comes with the regular USB connector.

Five-Watt Charging Adapter

The box comes with a five-watt charging adapter. While there are other charging blocks available in the market that offer a faster charge, the one that is in the box will offer the same charging speed as the previous ones released by Apple.

Ear Pods With A Lightning Connector

The 3.5mm headphone jack has been history ever since Apple introduced the iPhone 7 in 2016 and the case is the same as the new iPhone XR. The ear pods provided with the iPhone XR team up with the lightning connector to plug into the charging port offering access to music and other audio features. Since the connectors are not compatible with the universal 3.5mm connector, you are restricted to use the earpods with the iPhone.

Kindly note that the Ear Pods are not AirPods that cost $159 and are wireless in nature. We did expect Apple to introduce a newer version of the Ear Pods in their September 2018 conference, but there was no sign of any such launch at the event.

Another point to be noted is that Apple has not offered the dongle for the 3.5mm adapter to lightning cable in the box and you will need to get your own from Apple at $9 or from any 3rd party vendor. So if you don't have Bluetooth Earphones, or if you do not want to use the set that came bundled along in the box, you will have to shell out the extra dollars to reconnect your non-Apple headphones or earphones.

Overall Performance Notes

If your decision to purchase an iPhone was only based on benchmark scores, it is totally fine if you wonder why anyone would want to go for an iPhone XS and not purchase the iPhone XR. The performance is the same, the battery life is shorter and the damage to the pocket is $250 more.

However, the quality of an iPhone is determined by factors more than just benchmark scores. The iPhone XS has

1. High-resolution OLED display with HDR support

2. Dual rear cameras for portrait pictures

3. 3D touch

4. Better Waterproofing

5. More storage options

6. 4GB of RAM as compared to the 3GB on iPhone XR

The difference in RAM did not show much of an impact in the benchmark results but it will be something that will affect performance over the years.

The best thing about the iPhone XR is that its benchmarks, unlike iPhone 5C, which was the cheap model of that particular year, do not compromise on performance or battery despite being the cheapest model of 2018. Therefore, we can keep reiterating that the iPhone XR has had the best battery life an iPhone ever had. Therefore, there are very low chances of the iPhone XR becoming obsolete before the iPhone XS does.

Chapter 7: Initial Setup

Regardless of whether you are upgrading your iPhone for the latest iPhone XR or are a first-time Apple user, it is time to set up your new iPhone. The process of setting up the iPhone can be rather exhilarating, pretty much like waking up on Christmas morning and unwrapping all the presents placed under the Christmas tree. There are numerous features that you can explore, but before you can do this, you need to set up your iPhone. From the instant you see the first "Hello" displayed on your screen until the final step, here is everything that you must know about setting up your brand-new iPhone XR.

Different Options

When you are setting up your new iPhone, there are three options that you can use, and they are - starting over again, restoring the data from another iPhone, or even by importing the data from a non-iOS phone. If you wish to start anew, it means that you will need to set up your phone as a completely new device and must start changing all the settings. You must opt for this option if you have never used a smartphone before or you want to make it feel like your iPhone is brand-new, in a literal sense. You can restore the data that you have backed up on the iCloud or iTunes from any previous iOS backed device like an iPhone, iPad or even an iPod touch. You must opt for this if you are an existing iOS device user and are upgrading to the latest model of the iPhone. If you are a current user of a smartphone that's powered by Android, BlackBerry or Windows, then you might need to transfer all the data from your previous phone to your new iPhone XR.

Chapter 8: Start the Set-Up Process

As soon as you power up your iPhone for the first time, you will be greeted by a pleasant "Hello" on your screen in different languages. This one thing stays the same regardless of whether you are setting up your iPhone as a new device, are importing data from a non-iOS device, or are transferring the data from another iPhone.

> The first thing that you must do is place your finger on the "slide to set up" option on your screen and gently slide your finger across the iPhone's screen to start.

> Now, you need to select your language. Select a language of your choice from the extensive list that's displayed on your screen.

Once you do this, you must select your region or country.

The fourth step is to configure your network settings. You must opt for "Wi-Fi" network unless you are not within the range of a Wi-fFi network, then you can opt for the "Cellular" instead of "Wi-Fi network."

As soon as you do this, you have the option of setting up your iPhone XR using the passcode and settings you used on your previous iPhone. To do this, you must select the "Automatic Setup" option. If you want to set up your new iPhone XR as a brand-new device, then here are the steps that you can follow.

Once you read the Data and Privacy policies of Apple, please select "continue."

Click on "Enable Location Services." If you aren't interested in enabling the location services at the moment, you can click on the "Skip Location Services" option for now. You can enable these services later.

Now, it is time to create the Face ID for your iPhone XR. This is quite easy; you merely need to make sure that you can view your face in the circle that's displayed on the screen. Move your head around gradually to complete the circle. Once this is done, the device will inform you about it.

You need to set a Passcode for your new device. You can either use a regular 6-digit passcode, a 4-digit passcode, or even customize your passcode by selecting the "Passcode Options."

If you wish to start afresh, it means that you will need to set up your phone as a completely new device and must start changing all the settings. You must choose this option if you have never used a smartphone before or you want to make it feel like your iPhone is brand-new, in a literal sense. Here are the steps:

Set Up as a New iPhone → Apple ID and Password (You can easily create one by following the instructions displayed on your screen).

Read and then tap "Agree" to Apple's T&Cs.

Now, set up Apple Pay, iCloud Keychain, and Siri.

You can restore the data that you have backed up on the iCloud or iTunes from any previous iOS backed device like an iPhone, iPad or even iPod touch. You must opt for this if you are an existing iOS device user and are upgrading to the latest model of the iPhone. If you wish to restore your apps and data from another iPhone, then you have two options available - either use iCloud or iTunes. This choice depends on whether you used to backup your previous iPhone in iCloud or by plugging it to your computer and then backing it up using iTunes. Before you can choose either of these, ensure that your previous iPhone is backed up. Now, you merely need to determine whether you wish to restore data and apps using iCloud or iTunes.

If you are an existing user of a smartphone that's powered by Android, BlackBerry or Windows, then you might need to transfer all the data from your previous phone to your new iPhone XR. To do this, you must use an app provided by Apple known as "Move to iOS," and it is now available in the Google Play store. Before you can transfer the data to your iPhone, please download this app on your existing Android phone and follow the steps as the app guides you.

Chapter 9: iPhone XR Battery In Detail

This is probably the test you've wanted to see results for all along because this is where the iPhone XR produces interesting results. If you compared the iPhone XS to the iPhone Max, the battery consumption considered was fairly simple. The iPhone XS Max is the same phone like the iPhone XS which is just bigger in size and therefore comes with a battery which is 3174 mAh as compared to the 2658 mAh on the iPhone XS. The pixel density and the OLED technology stands the same on both the phones. The end result shows that the iPhone XS Max gets an additional hour of screen time in comparison with the iPhone XS.

As opposed to iPhone XS and XS Max, the iPhone XR is a completely different matter when it comes to battery life. The 6.1-inch display is the intermediate between the 5.8-inch screen of the XS and 6.5-inch screen of the XS Max. The battery with 2942 mAh also falls between the battery capacities of its siblings. But the difference is in the display as the iPhone XR comes with an LCD instead of an OLED like its siblings and has a pixel density of 326 pixels per inch which is less in comparison to its siblings which have a pixel density of 458 pixels per inch. The power utilization from the processor is the same as the other models but the iPhone XR saves battery on its display.

Something you will fancy about the iPhone XR is drawing comparisons with the XS and XS Max, especially since you are paying much less to get it.

Let's have a look at the battery. The XR features a 2,942 mAh battery. Of course, this comes nowhere close to the flagship iPhones with a battery capacity of more than 4,000 mAh. However, why is this important? Well, the XS only runs a 2,658 mAh battery. So, for a few bucks less, you are getting more juice out of the XR. The XS Max, however, features a 3,174 mAh battery.

The official battery specifications for the iPhone XR according to Apple are as follows:

Up to 25 hours talk time on wireless

Up to 15 hours on Internet use

Up to 16 hours video playback on wireless

Up to 65 hours audio playback on wireless

Compared to the iPhone 8 Plus, you have around one and a half hours more battery life, which makes it a good idea for someone who is looking for an upgrade.

Also, a bonus, Apple also included wireless charging on the iPhone XR.

Battery Life

iPhone XR: 333

iPhone XS: 264

iPhone XS Max: 314

iPhone X: 257

IDG

The iPhone XR has a battery that has proved to be the best among all the iPhones that exist in the market currently.

The test is not an ideal everyday scenario but an intensive power draining case where the screen is always on and the CPU and GPU are kept under continuous load. In an ideal scenario where you use it on a daily basis, you will end up getting much longer battery life than the results you see in this test, especially if the tasks and apps being used on the phone are simple. So this test does not serve as a perfect analogy to everyday use of the iPhone XR but helps you understand the difference in battery life as compared to the siblings of the iPhone X family.

The test between the iPhones of the X-family yielded the following results.

1. The iPhone XR lasted 19 minutes longer in comparison to the iPhone XS Max.

2. The iPhone XR lasted 60+ minutes longer than the iPhone XS.

In a real-world routine, where you are not purposely draining the battery life, the above result will translate to about 30-45 minutes of more screen time in comparison with the iPhone XS Max and around 2 hours more as compared to that of the iPhone XS, depending upon the usage pattern on your phone.

Thus, we can safely say that the iPhone XR holds a better charge than any other iPhone available in the market today.

An interesting test with the iPhone 7 showed the following results for the iPhone XR when we compared battery life.

1. The iPhone XR and the iPhone 7 have almost the same battery size, which is around 2900mAh.

2. Both of the phones have an LCD display with almost the same area. The display on the iPhone XR is 90 square centimeters while that on iPhone 7 is 83 square centimeters, which is only 7 percent smaller.

Even after such marginal differences, the iPhone XR lasted an hour and 45 minutes longer in the above-mentioned test.

This implies at least a 45 percent improvement in battery life from the iPhone 7 to the iPhone XR even after providing a larger display. This is a big achievement by Apple in a period of 2 years.

Chapter 10: Camera and Resolution in Detail

The camera is one of the key features a lot of people consider if they plan to buy an iPhone, and the iPhone XR is no different. The camera built into the iPhone XR is leveraged on the power of the A12 chip, delivering some fantastic capabilities.

You are getting a 7-megapixel selfie camera, which is the same specification used in the iPhone XS and iPhone XS Max. What you might not be able to enjoy, however, is the zoom feature. The picture quality is not as good as you would expect in an iPhone.

You have a 12-megapixel rear camera on the iPhone XR. All you can do with this camera is a digital zoom. The problem with cameras that are limited to digital zoom is that the quality can be grainy. This is a concern, especially when you compare the iPhone XR with iPhone XS and iPhone XS Max, which have a telephoto lens with optical zoom. The camera on the iPhone XR, however, gets saved by the A12 bionic chip. This powerful processor allows you to edit the depth of field in your photos after your shots.

The power behind the A12 bionic processor is responsible for the amazing graphics performance, real-time machine learning, and amazing photo processing capabilities that you get with the iPhone XR. This device also features an improved image signal processor and improved sensors. While it only has a 12 MP camera that has been a mainstay for many years, you can still enjoy detailed photos. With the Smart HDR function, you can improve your photos thanks to machine learning. Even though you only have one camera on the iPhone XR, you can still take decent photos in portrait mode.

The iPhone XR has a resolution of 1792 x 828 pixels, with a 326 ppi density. The iPhone XS, on the other hand, has a 2436 x 1125 resolution, and a 458 ppi. What this means is that with the iPhone XR, you can only enjoy watching videos up to 828p. This is good for most of the videos you can come across during your mobile experience. However, if you are looking to enjoy an unrivaled YouTube or Netflix experience on your iPhone XR, you might be slightly disappointed. You should, however, still be able to render most games on the iPhone without a hitch.

Here is a detailed report of how the single lens camera on the iPhone XR compares to all the other phone cameras in the world right now. We will deep dive into the iPhone XR camera and perform tests on the various features of the camera to see how good it is.

The iPhone XR offers a single-lens camera for photography, as opposed to the dual-lens setup that can be found on the iPhone XS models. If we look at the specifications of the camera on the iPhone XR, it gives us exactly what one can expect from a top of the line, single lens device featuring the following.

12MP

A 1/2.55″ sensor which has a 1.4µm pixel pitch

26mm f/1.8 aperture lens which comes along with optical image stabilization

Dual Tone LED Flash

Phase-detection autofocus (PDAF)

4K videos at 24/30/60 fps (1080p at 30 fps at default settings)

Although there is a difference in hardware of the camera, when we look at the image processing and the software side of things, the iPhone XR is equipped with the same technology as the iPhone XS models.

A professional camera, when capturing stills, tends to capture a multi-frame buffer using different exposures, which facilitates zero lag on the shutter and HDR processing. This technology is available on the latest iPhones including the iPhone XR and therefore it has the ability to display HDR image on your screen in real time. This simply means that you end up getting a preview image true to the saying "what you see is what you get."

DxOMark Tests

DxOMark is a website providing image quality ratings for standalone cameras, lenses, and mobile devices that include cameras, particularly smartphones. Let's go through the rating DxOMark provided for the single-lens camera on the iPhone XR.

Exposure and Contrast: 90

The iPhone XR gets a good exposure score since it provides a wide dynamic range through both indoor and outdoor conditions along with accurate exposures. If the lighting is very bright with an increase in contrast scenes, the HDR triggers automatically in the default mode of the camera resulting in capturing detailed pictures in both the darkest and brightest regions. The HDR results on the iPhone XR are at par with that of the iPhone XS Max, having a slight difference, but still, the iPhone XR retains more highlight fractionally as compared to the Pixel 2 by Google.

The iPhone XR provides excellent target exposures even at very low light at 20 lux. The target exposure is a little less than ideal when the light conditions drop down to very low such as 1 to 5 lux, but you will still get images that are very usable. The iPhone XS Max provides marginally better target exposure even at 1 lux, which is why it gets an upper hand over its sibling in the exposure department.

The iPhone XR is very good with exposure of faces even when there is a lot of background light, proving that the image processing algorithms work as intended.

Target exposure is almost accurate indoors where the lighting is accompanied with good contrast and details are preserved well through the highlight in the regions with shadow.

Color: 82

The iPhone XR ends up rendering vibrant and saturated colors, especially in outdoor lighting conditions, resulting in the hues really popping up. In low light conditions, colors remain subtle but are still pleasant to the eyes.

The color saturation remains very good in low light shots at around 20 lux and is just a tad bit behind the Pixel 2 and the iPhone XS Max. The Pixel 2 has a white balance that looks greener under fluorescent lighting which makes its white look cleaner but the iPhone XR has warmer tones which make the image look naturally attractive in the indoors.

The white balance on the iPhone XR camera

is mostly accurate in all lighting conditions and does not show any odd colors even when shot with artificial sources of light such as the flash. In outdoor conditions, the white balance of the iPhone XR is a little more biased toward the colder blue tone whereas it remains on the warm side in indoor conditions, but remains very acceptable under both conditions.

Autofocus: 99

The autofocus on the iPhone XR is excellent as one would expect from high-end devices, which are equipped with Phase Detection Auto Focus (PDAF). Benchmark tests conducted under controlled lab environments showed that the iPhone XR was consistent in finding focus accurately and fast as well. During the test, the iPhone XR was exposed to defocusing between clicking images, keeping intervals of 500ms to 2000ms before requesting focus again and the iPhone XR surprised everyone as it still managed to focus and click sharp images and never failed to click a shot on autofocus. This procedure was repeated under a variety of lighting conditions and the results were consistent every time.

The zero shutter lag technology on the iPhone XR camera, which keeps buffering the frames while the camera app is on ensures that the camera clicks the exact same picture as you would see in the display at a given instance in time.

Texture: 75 Noise: 69

The iPhone XR features the same texture versus noise ratio as that of the iPhone XS Max. The recorded Accutane is over 80 percent when the camera is used in outdoor conditions, and the detail in still images is amazing. The details in static scenes remain very good even in low light conditions. The acutance is still recorded to be around 60 percent even in extreme low light conditions for static captures. If you are using a shutter speed of slower than 1/40 second in low light conditions of 20 lux or below, using the hand as well as the tripod will lead to a loss in detail in frames where there is a movement of the subject, where the acutance will be 1 lux for such images. You don't need to worry as this is acceptable behavior, and overall the iPhone XR does a wonderful job with its camera at capturing details.

Artifacts: 86

The iPhone XR scores low on artifacts for its flaws in image quality and optical deficiencies. The iPhone XR has the following areas of concern.

Moiré effect in high-frequency patterns

Ringing

Flare in shots that have a backlight

Minor color quantization

Ringing in the iPhone XR has been visible during high contrast edges in HDR shots.

An example would be the visible railing in a bright sky. But if you are not printing the image out or viewing it on a large resolution, this can be neglected as it can be considered to be marginal to the overall quality of the image.

The moiré effect is a phenomenon that causes a rainbow appearing in your picture along the high-frequency areas of the shot where the resolution of your iPhone is not sufficient to capture fine details.

Flash: 83

The Flash on the iPhone XR gives better performance as compared to the iPhone XS Max since it provides better target exposure for faces and also in the center of the frame. We will not say that it is perfect as there is still evidence of flash only shots when the exposure is low but the algorithms on iPhone XR are definitely better than the iPhone XS Max for the Flash. You may see some vignette effects along the corner which are visible. The level of detail is good on Flash but there are some color quantization and residual noise, using both mixed lights and flash only shots. We can call it to be an improvement in the flash from the past iPhone models, but it is still not at par with a Google Pixel 2, which can be crowned as the king of Flash.

Zoom: 35

The image quality of the iPhone XR primary camera is as good as that of its elder siblings from the iPhone XS range. However, the single-camera setup on the iPhone XR fails to amaze for bokeh and zoom shots, where the dual camera setup of the iPhone XS and XS Max get an advantage. Using up to 2x zoom on the iPhone XR delivers images that are acceptable in both outdoor and indoor shots.

However, the difference between the single-camera setup and the dual camera setup becomes very visible when the zoom range is increased. If you increase the zoom range to 4x, you will notice that the iPhone XS Max preserves intricate details, such as the railings of a bridge. Although, the iPhone XR scores a little bit more in zoom detailing compared to the Google Pixel 2.

At medium range zoom of 4x and long-range zoom of 8x, the noise of the iPhone XR along with some artifacts like aliasing becomes very prevalent. Detail is still acceptable in bright conditions outdoors, and indoor shots to some extent as well, but do not expect to find fine details such as lines on brickwork or text on signboards when you are using the long-range zoom on your iPhone XR.

It is all right to admit that the iPhone XR's zoom is very limited compared to the iPhone XS or Google Pixel 2. Zooming to maximum magnification on the iPhone XR camera does not produce the same results like that on the iPhone XS or a Google Pixel 2. Nevertheless, for a single camera device, the iPhone XR gives a decent performance that is almost at par with the Google Pixel 2 but falls short of competing with the tele-lens zoom on the iPhone XS and XS Max.

Bokeh: 35

The quality of images in portrait mode also suffers a bit due to the absence of the tele-lens in the iPhone XR. The iPhone XR primary camera with its wide view comes with a 26mm lens, which is not exactly the best thing for portraits. You may try to get the subject into the frame by moving closer but you will observe that the facial features will undergo some distortion, anamorphosis, and especially on elements which are closer to the frame's edge.

The portrait mode in the iPhone XR works well on human subjects shot in low-light settings, resulting in getting better details on the face as compared to the iPhone XS, provided that the distance between the camera and the subject is less. Facial detail is perhaps the iPhone XR's best feature, and even though the bokeh effect helps separate the subject in the foreground from the background, we can't exactly call it perfect. The iPhone XR's camera in the absence of the tele-lens fails to calculate depth, resulting into the visibility of subject masking artifacts ultimately making the portrait look like a photoshopped cut-out where the subject was placed into the background.

The Bokeh test by DxOMark is for both still objects and humans. As we have already discussed above, the iPhone XR's portrait mode works well with subjects with a face. The algorithm uses face detection, and therefore when used with still objects, the algorithm fails to trigger the bokeh effect leading to only the optical bokeh, which has very low efficiency. This is where the iPhone XR loses a few points to rival smartphones that are good with applying the bokeh effect to still objects as well. When the iPhone XR cannot detect a face in the frame while using the portrait mode, you will be prompted with a "no face detected" message.

Video Scores

DxOMark gives the iPhone XR and an excellent score of 96 points on Video because of its ability to capture beautifully in bright light environments. The final score is derived from a number of scores from the individual parameters such as:

Color: 88

Exposure: 88

Autofocus: 92

Noise: 77

Texture: 57

Stabilization: 94

Artifacts: 84

The iPhone XR, overall, stands at par with the iPhone XS Max in terms of videography in outdoor videos with color rendering and the white balance being very good, and stabilization being excellent as well in slow motion. There are small instabilities with respect to exposure and white balance under inconsistent lighting scenarios. The level of detail is low on the iPhone XR when compared with the iPhone XS Max in low light conditions, but the noise is not much visible. This implies that Apple has worked its algorithm to strike a balance between noise and sharpness at a budget price.

The target exposure while capturing videos with an iPhone XR is very good in all possible lighting conditions down to 20 lux. The videos may come out dark when shot in extremely low light through 1 to 10 lux, but they are still pretty usable. Change in exposure while shooting in changing light is also good, with the transition time being negligible.

The white balance and color rendering work well through both indoor and outdoor conditions, and the level of saturation might go in low light, but it stays more than acceptable even in low light conditions.

The iPhone XR also impresses with texture preservation again through both indoor and outdoor videos. Although the texture suffers in low light, the noise to detail ratio is well managed. The iPhone XR preserves text and edges higher in indoor videos at 100 lux and even better in outdoor videos between 300 to 1000 lux.

The iPhone XR's autofocus works like a charm with videos just like it does with still pictures. This is because the iPhone XR is well balanced bundled with good response time and does not have any instabilities, jerkiness or overshoots that would disrupt the experience. The auto-focus works well in bright-light outdoor videos and the smoothness and tracking of the autofocus work efficiently too. The experience does not turn out to be as good in low-light environments but is still decent enough. The stabilization is consistent in all lighting conditions, frame sharpness is impressive and the videos tend to stay stable even when light conditions change. Motions related to panning and walking are controlled nicely too.

Best Single-lens Phone

The iPhone XR will be easily the most desired model of iPhones for Apple patrons who wish to upgrade their iPhones, given the rocketing price of the iPhone XS series launched a month before it. The single-cam implementation on the iPhone XR is what makes it very affordable, but this also means that you will have to compromise on some better features which are only bundled with the dual-cam XS series such as zoom and bokeh functions.

Apple has comfortably integrated the same software and image processing algorithms as that available in the iPhone XS series, and therefore the iPhone XR is at par with the functional capabilities of the iPhone XS and iPhone XS Max in many ways -- amazing exposure under all lighting conditions and an even better noise to detail ratio. The autofocus function also works well in all conditions.

The one place where the iPhone XR fails compared to its siblings in the X series is where the additions of a second camera with an extra sensor bundled with a tele-lens comes into the picture. So it would be naive to expect the same quality on zoom and bokeh effects The Portrait mode also looks a little bit artificial compared to the smooth portrait on the iPhone XS and XS Max.

The iPhone XR however, due to its better results for noise artifacts, take a spot over the Google Pixel 2 and becomes the best single-cam smartphone in the market.

Pros and Cons of the iPhone XR Camera

Pros

Provides a dynamic range on exposure in indoor and bright light conditions

Preserves detail well in all lighting conditions

Colors achieved are vivid and pleasant

Autofocus is accurate and fast

Optimized image stabilization

Cons

Detail preservation is low in medium to long range zoom shots

Noise and fine grain luminance is visible in low-light shots

Bokeh mode is not realistic

Instability of white balance while indoors

The iPhone XR camera is bang for the buck. The software and image processing offers the same camera experience as that provided by the iPhone XS and XS Max, with the biggest and only difference being the telephoto lens on the iPhone XS series. Apple has shown its strengths through the amazing camera experience, which has been very consistent among all the smartphones of the current generation. It also provides a leading quality in pictures that stands at par with all the competition in the market. The iPhone XR performs well on low-light and although it does not match the picture quality of its elder siblings with the dual-cam setup, it still manages to leave the Google Pixel 2 behind it in terms of camera and picture quality in the single-cam setup.

Chapter 11: Setting Up Your iPhone XR in Detail

Once you get your hands on your new iPhone XR, you are probably excited about firing it up and enjoying what it has to offer. Here are some features that will get you buzzing right away:

Face ID – allows you to confirm mobile payments and unlock your phone with ease, so setting this up right away will be a good idea.

Because the traditional physical home button no longer exists on the iPhone XR, you will want to learn how to do simple things like closing apps, taking screenshots, turning off the device and switching between the apps you are using.

Once you have the device out of the box, you can set it up in the following ways:

As a new device, a fresh installation without restoring any old settings from previous phones.

Restore old photos, music, apps, and anything else from a cloud backup or a backup in your iTunes account.

Restore data from an Android device.

Backup of the Old iPhone

If you own an iPhone already, there's a checklist of things you will need to create before you switch to the new iPhone XR. This chapter will help you transition as smoothly as possible from your current iPhone to your new iPhone XR.

Consider the following checklist during your move from your old iPhone to the new one.

This is a very important step while you migrate from your old iPhone to the new iPhone XR. You need to ensure that you have backed up all necessary data in the correct manner so that it becomes easy to later transfer it onto your new iPhone.

The easiest method to achieve this backup is by using iCloud.

You will need to navigate to Settings>>Apple ID>>iCloud and then use the toggle buttons and toggle everything you need to be backed up to "on."

Now scroll down to the iCloud Backup option and tap on "Back Up Now."

You may realize now that you need more space and this would be a good time to purchase a new iCloud storage plan. To do so, tap back and get into the iCloud settings, scroll to the top and get into Manage Storage. You can check your storage tier option here and purchase a plan accordingly.

Voilà! That is it and you are ready with your data backup. You can restore all this data onto your new iPhone XR while setting it up on first boot.

iTunes Backup

Power on the device and select your country and language. Your iPhone XR will prompt you to either restore settings from a backup, move data from your old Android device, or to set up your iPhone XR as a new phone.

Choose "Restore from an iTunes backup."

Use the provided Lightning to USB cable that comes with your device and connect it to your computer. In case your MacBook only has USB Type C ports, you must buy the Lightning to USB Type C cable.

If iTunes does not open automatically, open it, and you will be asked to allow the computer to access iPhone settings and information. Your iPhone will prompt you to accept whether you trust the connected computer.

On your iPhone, tap Trust, and on your computer, click Continue.

You will get a greeting message on the iPhone. Click Continue and Get Started.

Choose your iPhone on the list of devices that you can see on the left panel. Click on the iPhone summary tab. This tab should provide information on the type of device you are using, and useful information about the backups you have.

Select Restore Backup. In case you had saved backups for different devices, you can look at the time stamp to determine which of the backups is the most recent.

After restoring the backup, sync the iPhone XR to your computer, and then eject the drive.

iCloud Backup

Power on your iPhone XR and choose your country and language. You will be asked to choose how you want to set up the device, either from an Android device, as a new iPhone, or to restore settings and data from a backup.

Choose iCloud backup.

Enter the login details for your Apple ID account.

If you have turned on two-factor authentication, you should get an alert on any of your devices that are running iOS 10 or advanced models, or your MacBook, if it is running macOS Sierra or advanced models like macOS High Sierra and macOS Mojave.

Enter the code provided on your iPhone. Read and agree to the terms and conditions.

Look through the iCloud backups that you have, and going by the time stamp, choose the most recent.

Once you have selected the desired backup, decide whether you want to customize your settings on your new iPhone XR, or if you want to replicate the same settings you had on the old iPhone.

Your iPhone XR will then restore settings from the chosen iCloud backup.

Remember that this process might take a while, depending on how strong your Internet connection is. You can step away for a cup of coffee while you wait.

Chapter 12: The First Boot

Let's get you through the first boot on your new iPhone XR. You will be greeted with the Apple logo followed by a sweet Hello when you boot up the phone for the first time. You can then select your preferred language followed by your country or region. This will set up the language of your new iPhone over a few seconds.

You will then be directed to the "Quick Start" screen from where you start setting up your customizations on the iPhone. Tap on "Set Up Manually."

Naturally, the first thing the iPhone will ask you to do is set up and connect to your Home Wi-Fi network. Once you have set up the Wi-Fi on your iPhone, it may take a few minutes for the phone to be ready. Next, continue to accept Apple's Data and Privacy Policy and we then move on to set up your

Face ID. Fix your face in the frame of the camera and move your face in different angles to complete setting up your Face ID. If you choose to set up the Face ID later, you will be prompted to keep a passcode instead. The phone will then continue setting up your Apple ID followed by these configurations.

Automatic Updates: You can click on continue to configure Automatic Updates or you can click on "Install Updates Manually."

Location Services: Click on "Enable Location Services" as this will switch on the GPS services and help with day-to-day applications like Uber and Maps.

Apple Pay: If you have your Credit Card handy, you can set up your Apple Pay details for purchases.

iCloud Keychain: Your password management system, which can be enabled with the help of another Apple device.

Siri: Set up Siri, your AI-powered personal

assistant who is at your service to help you with all your needs.

Screen Time: Manage your time on the screen better by setting up Screen Time, which will give you weekly reports of time you spend on the phone. It will also allow you to set screen time limits for apps you want to cut down on.

iPhone Analytics: You can choose to share or not share statistics of your iPhone usage with Apple.

True Tone Display: A feature that lets the iPhone adjust to the light of its current environment such that colors appear to be consistent to you.

Display Zoom: Customize the kind of view you would like on your new iPhone XR using the options in this feature.

That is it and your iPhone is ready to use!

New Gestures

If you are upgrading from the iPhone X, you will already be familiar with most of the gestures on the iPhone XR as well. However, if you are coming from an iPhone 8 model or before, the following gestures and commands will help you ease your way into your new iPhone XR.

Notification Center: You can get to the Notification Center by swiping down from the top of the screen.

Home Screen: Swiping up on the home bar will land you on the home screen of your iPhone XR.

Control Center: Swiping down from the top right of the screen will get you to the Control Center.

Switching between Apps: If you want to switch between different open apps on the phone, you will need to swipe up and continue the swipe by performing a curved motion towards the right of the screen.

Siri: Swiping down from the center of the screen will activate your assistant to help you with your needs or even if you are in the mood to just hear a joke.

Reachability: Reachability is an iPhone feature introduced since iPhone 6 to shrink the screen size to smaller than the actual physical size of the display so that people with smaller hands can easily move their finger across the screen. Swiping down from just above the home bar will help you activate this feature.

Accessibility: The Accessibility feature in the iPhone allows you to set up voice commands for people who have challenges with respect to their vision. You can find the accessibility feature by triple tapping the side button.

Power-Off/SOS: Pressing and holding down the volume buttons simultaneously along with the power button will get you to the SOS mode.

Screenshot: To take a quick screenshot of your current screen, press the power button simultaneously along with the volume down button.

High-Efficiency Formats on your iPhone XR

Apple devices are equipped with software that is excellent with image compression and enabling this has a lot of benefits for your iPhone's camera.

Enabling this leads to almost 50 percent compression in size of the photos and videos while still retaining their high quality.

You can set this up by navigating to

Settings>>Camera>>Formats>>High Efficiency.

This is a must-have for anyone who is into clicking a lot of pictures and videos.

Setting up Safari Autofill and Face ID

We already spoke about the first boot up of

your iPhone XR where you get to set up your Face ID. If you skipped that to be set up later, this is how you can set it up.

Navigate to

Settings>>Face ID and Passcode>>Set up Face ID.

You will have to face the camera and position your face in the circle on the screen, which resembles a head. You will then have to move your face in different angles such that maximum parts are registered. Your phone will confirm when the process is complete.

Once the Face ID is set up, you can proceed to select which apps and feature you want to be secured by Face ID. It is advisable to select everything including Password Autofill.

You also get the choice to set up an alternate appearance for yourself. This feature helps to make the facial recognition system versatile. So if you wear glasses, you can set up a facial ID with the glasses on, or it can actually be used to set up facial recognition for another person who you'd like to have access to the same phone.

You can turn off this feature known as attention awareness, which needs you to look at the screen before unlocking it. Switching it off will speed up the process of Face ID authentication but will add another step of security.

Setting up Safari Autofill is simple and you just need to ensure that iCloud Keychain is on in your iCloud settings.

Navigate to

Settings>>Passwords and Accounts>>Switch Autofill Passwords to enable.

Now go to Safari settings and select Autofill. Here, you can select your information, and enable the contact info Autofill.

You can also enter your credit card details to be used for payment pages.

You can now surf the web pages on the Internet on Safari and when you fill any information in forms, you will be prompted to save the information in Keychain. The iOS 12 upgrade also allows users to integrate third-party application like 1Password and Dashlane to manage their passwords.

Display Settings Customization

One of the things you need to do when you get your new iPhone XR is to set up the display so that you have a good experience with the colors.

Navigate to

Settings>>Display and Brightness.

Here, you will be able to customize the way your iPhone's display reacts to different environments.

1. Disable "Raise to Wake" if you don't want the screen to come on automatically when you raise your phone.

2. You can also change the auto-lock period to something other than the default 30 seconds.

3. You can use the "Night Shift" feature to schedule and customize your phone usage in the night so that it doesn't keep you up at night.

4. You can disable "True Tone" which is a feature that turns the screen in a paper-white tone in any lighting environment.

You can also enable or disable the Auto Brightness feature from

Settings>>General>>Accessibility>>Displa y Accommodations.

Control Center Customization

The Control Center on your new iPhone XR will look pretty bland and empty since there's not much that has been added to it.

Navigate to

Settings>>Control   Center>>Customize Controls.

Here, you can add or remove controls for Notes, Apple TV Remote, Screen Recording, etc.

To add features, tap the green "+" sign to add them. You can remove them by tapping the red "-" sign and can arrange them by pressing on them and dragging them.

Protecting Your New iPhone XR

Lastly, we would advise you to purchase AppleCare+. If not, we suggest that you get a good screen protector and cover.

AppleCare+ has made a number of changes to its policies and you have up to 60 days after your iPhone purchase to decide whether you want AppleCare or not.

You can find many screen protectors and cases for your iPhone on Amazon for reasonable costs. However, if you are looking to purchase the best one, we recommend going for the ones directly provided by Apple.

Chapter 13: Network and Connectivity

Selecting a Network

You get 2 options when you insert a SIM in your iPhone XR. Either you can let it choose a network automatically or you can select a manual network for it.

Navigate to

Settings>>Mobile Data>>Mobile Network.

1. Automatic>>Toggle it to be On or Off.

2. If you are keeping it off, proceed further by selecting your desired network manually.

Press Mobile Data to save the setting.

Selecting a Network Mode

This option basically lets you decide which

network modes your iPhone XR is allowed to use. Depending on that, your phone will achieve Internet speeds respectively.

Navigate to

Settings>>Mobile Data>>Mobile Data Options>>Enable 4G.

1. Off

2. Voice and Data

3. Data only

The 4G network can be used for voice calls through the mobile network, which results in a better and faster connection. If you deactivate 4G, your iPhone will automatically connect to 3G or 2G depending on availability.

Data on the 4G network is faster than that of 3G or 2G as well. An ideal 4G network can handle download speeds between 5 to 12 Mbps, upload speeds up to 5 Mbps, and can reach peak download speeds up to 50 Mbps.

Connecting to WLAN (Wi-Fi or Wireless network)

WLAN can be used as an alternative to using the mobile network when you want to connect to the Internet. When you're connected to the Internet using WLAN, your iPhone XR won't make use of mobile data.

Navigate to Settings>>Press Wi-Fi>>Toggle Wi-Fi to On.

A list of available Wi-Fi networks will be displayed. Select the network you are familiar with and key in the password to connect to the Wi-Fi Network.

Activate/Deactivate Mobile Data

You can limit the use of mobile data by deactivating it when it's not absolutely essential. This would ensure no connectivity to the Internet via the mobile network. You can still connect to the Internet using WLAN when the mobile data is deactivated.

Navigate to

Settings>>Mobile Data>>Toggle Mobile Data to On/Off.

Alternatively, if you want to restrict only particular apps from using mobile data, you could do so by scrolling down and toggling mobile data off for the required app.

Activate/Deactivate Data Roaming

When you are traveling outside your country of residence, the network provider who you have purchased the SIM from might not be offering services in the country you are traveling to. In such cases, your phone automatically latches on to an available network, which is known as Roaming. Similarly, roaming can get applied to your Data as well but it will cost you a lot of money if your plan does not support international roaming at reasonable costs. Thus it is always a wise choice to turn off data roaming while you are traveling. You can still always connect to an available WLAN network while you are in another country.

To turn off Data Roaming, navigate to

Settings>>Mobile Data>>Mobile Data options>>Data Roaming>>Toggle it to Off.

Using your iPhone XR as your Personal Hotspot

When you use your phone as a Personal Hotspot, you can use your phone's Internet connection to be shared wirelessly (WLAN) among other devices such as another phone or a laptop.

To set up a hotspot on your iPhone XR, navigate to

Settings>>Personal Hotspot>>Toggle it to On.

Set up a password of your choice to allow access to only people you want to give access to.

There are 3 options through which other devices can connect to your Hotspot.

1. Using Wi-Fi

2. Using Bluetooth

3. Using USB

Click on Done and you have set up your Personal Hotspot.

Activate/Deactivate GPS

Your iPhone XR can determine your location geographically by using the GPS (Global Positioning System). This information about your location is used by numerous apps on your iPhone such as Maps, Uber, etc.

To turn GPS off, navigate to

Settings>>Privacy>>Location Services>>Toggle it to Off.

If you leave it on, you also get options to manage GPS specifically for individual apps as well.

Chapter 14: iPhone XR Benchmarks

When the iPhone XS and iPhone XS Max were launched in September 2018, they met the expectation of the masses: they were not only the most performing iPhones ever made, but they were the fastest smartphones in the world. The A12 Bionic chip by Apple had crushed every other processor ever manufactured for a smartphone.

The iPhone XR is available with the A12 Bionic chip pumping its veins with the same adrenaline and is expected to deliver the same high-powered performance as its siblings. Also, given that the iPhone XR is big on battery life and low on resolution, which is 1792 x 828 pixels, it is expected to have a battery life, which lasts longer than any other iPhone in the market.

So if you live in a world where you only care about benchmarks, you simply need to get the cheapest iPhone of 2018. Let's see where the most popular benchmark tests place the iPhone XR in comparison to its sibling from the iPhone X family.

Geekbench 4

Geekbench is preferred by most techies for benchmarking devices because of its cross-platform availability for platforms such as Windows, iOS, Linux and Android. There is no benchmark test available in the market that can be called the perfect one across platforms but Geekbench 4 is the closest we can get.

The Geekbench 4 benchmark produced the following results for iPhone XR when compared with the iPhone XS and XS Max.

Compute Metal Performance

iPhone XR: 22025

iPhone XS: 21574

iPhone XS Max: 21967

iPhone X: 15691

CPU - Multi Core

iPhone XR: 11326

iPhone XS: 11382

iPhone XS Max: 11096

iPhone X: 10377

CPU - Single Core

iPhone XR: 4818

iPhone XS: 4807

iPhone XS Max: 4813

iPhone X: 4253

As we can see from the score, the iPhone XR is at par with the XS and XS Max with just a high or low of a few percentage points.

If we look at the single-core performance, it

is 13 percent faster than iPhone X and about 10 percent faster in multi-core performance.

The performance of the iPhone XR also stands at 40 percent better than the iPhone X in the GPU powered compute metal test.

AnTuTu V7

Known for its popularity in the world of Android smartphones, AnTuTu is also available on iOS. The test produced different and varying results on every run when tried on the latest version of AnTuTu. So, it's not necessary to stress on these numbers but here are the results to satisfy everyone's curiosity.

GPU

iPhone XR: 142593

iPhone XS: 103170

iPhone XS Max: 117224

iPhone X: 20148

CPU

iPhone XR: 120183

iPhone XS: 115313

iPhone XS Max: 121849

iPhone X:103221

Overall

iPhone XR:335174

iPhone XS:305409

iPhone XS Max: 309188

iPhone X: 244204

It is surprising that the iPhone XR score more than the XS and XS Max in the GPU test, thus boosting its overall score. The reason for this is probably the low-resolution scheme on the iPhone XR display. The tests are rendered and performed on-screen and a fixed or off-screen resolution is avoided. The A12 Bionic chip delivers faster frames on the iPhone XR because the number of pixels to be rendered on iPhone XS and iPhone XS Max are 85 percent and 125 percent more respectively.

3DMark

3DMark is the favorite test for determining the graphics performance of everyone in the tech world.

There is a Slingshot version of the 3DMark test that runs a graphic intensive test, which is almost like a real game. It then delivers the test results based on the performance.

Sling Shot Extreme

    iPhone XR: 3602

    iPhone XS: 3557

    iPhone XS Max: 3595

    iPhone X: 3568

Sling Shot Extreme Unlimited

    iPhone XR: 4297

iPhone XS: 3955

iPhone XS Max:4067

iPhone X: 3925

Given that the 3DMark test runs at a fixed resolution, the iPhone XR delivers almost the same performance as that of an iPhone XS and an iPhone XS Max.

The test is run on two different versions.

1. Sling Shot Extreme runs the test using the Metal API provided by Apple which starts at a resolution of 2560 x 1440 but is later scaled higher or lower as per the resolution of the device it is being tested on.

2. Sling Shot Extreme Unlimited performs the same test off-screen.

Note: neither of the tests is affected by the lower resolution of the iPhone XR.

The results of the iPhone XR are at par with that of the XS or XS Max, and also almost identical to that of the iPhone X. Apple had claimed that the A12 Bionic chip will up the graphics performance by 50 percent; however, this is not the case as seen from the results where the iPhone X is at par with the XR, XS, and XS Max. We believe this has happened because the test is also largely dependent on the memory and cache performance of the device over just the GPU performance.

We, therefore, do a simple Ice Storm test to see if it proves our theory. This test runs a simple scene like a game by implementing OpenGL ES 2.0 through a fixed resolution of 1280 x 720 resulting in all devices rendering the exact same frames.

CPU - Multi-Core

iPhone XR: 77344

iPhone XS: 75528

iPhone XS Max: 77022

iPhone X: 64382

As this test is less stressful on the processor, it demands less memory and cache. Therefore as seen from the results, it runs 18 percent faster on an A12 chip compared to that on an A11 chip.

Chapter 15: iPhone XR Tips and Tricks in Detail

The iPhone XR is a unique device in the line of iPhone products. Retailing below $1,000, it is the first device that has Face ID and an edge-to-edge design. This is a device that is simply designed for use by everyone. Whether you are upgrading from an iPhone 6 or an iPhone 8, this is the device you should run to.

There is a lot that you can learn to help you get the utmost utility from this device. It might take you a while to get used to the tweaks, but once you do, this will be one of the best mobile experiences you have had in years. The following are some useful tips that will help you make the most use of your phone.

Waking your Phone Up

Unlike the previous devices, iPhone XR has a Tap to Wake feature. If you do not want to fiddle with the side button, tap on the screen and it will wake up. This is ideal if you want to check notifications and get back to whatever you were doing.

Accessing Home

The Home button is conspicuously missing in the iPhone XR. To access Home, swipe up on your screen from the bottom. This gesture will also unlock your iPhone XR.

App Switcher

To access App Switcher, swipe up from your Home bar, but hold on briefly. However, for an on-the-go user, this is a waste of time. Instead of doing this, swipe up on your screen from the left edge at 45 degrees. This gets you to the App Switcher.

Accessing the Notification Center

To view your notifications from the notification center, swipe down from the notch area.

Accessing Control Center

Swipe down from either the right ear or right edge close to the notch to access the Control Center. From here, you can customize settings as you please to include settings for Accessibility, your Apple TV remote, and so forth.

Making Payments

Using Apple Pay for payments is very easy. Press your side button twice – it is on the right side of the phone. Hold your iPhone XR to your face and use Face ID to scan your face.

Switching between Recent Apps

The iPhone XR comes with a Quick App

switcher gesture. With this, you can switch between your recent apps seamlessly. To access an app you used previously, swipe right. Keep swiping to access the apps further. A left swipe takes you back to the app you accessed first.

This only works if you do not interact with any app. If you do, the system detects this, and you have to swipe right to access the one you were using previously. This is a simple process, but it can be confusing. You will need some practice to familiarize yourself with it.

Taking Screenshots

You do not have a Home button on the iPhone XR, so taking a screenshot the traditional way is not possible. For screenshots, press and hold the volume down button and the lock button.

Using Siri

The easiest way to access Siri is to press and

hold the lock button. Alternatively, if you are not comfortable with this setting, you can set up Hey Siri for additional functionality.

Rebooting your device

The lack of a home button makes some mundane tasks on the iPhone seem complicated, like rebooting your phone. Hold the lock button and any of the volume buttons to reboot your device.

Perform a hard reset

There is nothing special about a hard reset. It is but an elevated reboot. In case you were wondering, a hard reset does not erase data from your phone. Press volume up, volume down, then press and hold the hold button until the Apple logo appears on your screen.

Creating Memojis

Emojis have been delightful highlights to many conversations. With the Face ID and the TrueDepth camera on the iPhone XR, you get to animate your emojis and make conversations more entertaining. The Memoji is an advanced form of emoji that is more fun to work with. When using a Memoji, you are creating a Bitmoji-like character on your phone. To create a Memoji, go to Messages, choose any iMessage chat and click on the Animoji app, then proceed.

Depth Effect Selfies

Having an iPhone with an amazing camera sensor is a good thing. You are able to take amazing selfies with depth effect. On your camera, change to portrait mode and flip your iPhone XR for this unique selfie.

Managing Notifications from your Lock Screen

The iOS 12 brings advanced user abilities to the iPhone XR. From your lock screen, you can access and manage notifications. To do this, swipe left on any notification notice and tap Manage.

This is where you can turn off notifications for apps that you do not need to receive frequently. Other settings include Deliver Quietly, where the app does not show notifications on your lock screen. Your phone will not make a sound if the app has any notifications. However, to access such notifications, you must open the Notification Center.

Two-Pane Landscape View

The two-pane landscape view is characteristic of the iPhone XS Max. Apple also introduced this in the iPhone XR. On your phone, perhaps you are accessing Mail, and you also need to keep track of some notes, just flip your phone to the side, and you will get the same two-pane view that you should be familiar with when using an iPad.

Face ID Fails

As amazing as Face ID is, at times it becomes a bother when it gets wonky. If you try to initiate Face ID and it fails, you can give it a second try. Do not enter your passcode just yet, instead, swipe up and you will get the settings right.

Multiple Face ID Faces

iOS 12 allows you to register more than one face for Face ID. Perhaps you need to share your phone with your partner, so this would come in handy. All you need to do is add a second face to your Face ID settings.

Go to Settings, select Face ID, then Set Up an Alternative Appearance. Your iPhone XR will give you prompts to follow, until you are done setting up a second face.

Bring back the Home Button

While some people have made peace with the fact that the Home Button is no more, others cannot move on that easily. If swipe gestures to enjoy Home Button services are not your thing, you can use the AssistiveTouch Home Button. This is a virtual feature that allows you to bring back the home button.

Go to Settings, then Accessibility, and select AssistiveTouch. From here, you can create shortcuts for 3D Touch, long press, single tap, and double tap. You can define unique gestures for different responses.

Editing Depth from Portrait Shots

Your iPhone XR might only come with one camera, but this does not limit you from getting the most out of it. Having taken photos, you can still edit them later on with depth effect. In photo view, tap on edit and use the slider at the bottom of the screen to alter the depth effect as you desire.

Setting up Fast Charge

The iPhone XR comes with a 5W charger. For someone who uses their phone all the time, it will run out of juice. The iPhone XR supports a fast charge, so a fast charger will come in handy. If you have an iPad, you can use your 12W charger for your iPhone XR.

Taking RAW photos

The default iPhone camera is decent as it is. You can do so much with it, without any added settings. However, if you need full control of things like shutter speed, focus, and exposure, you must install a third-party application. One of the best for this is Halide, which allows you to take RAW photos.

Shortcuts for task automation

The iPhone XR is one of the smartest devices you will ever get in the market at the moment. Some tasks, especially repetitive ones, can be automated. You can also group others together. The Shortcuts app helps you create shortcuts that can, among other things, send messages, read headlines, change the Do Not Disturb mode, turn off the lights and so forth, all with a single command.

Water Resistance

In a market that has a lot of phones that are capable of doing amazing things underwater, the iPhone XR is not one of them. This is an IP67 phone, which means that it is only splash resistant. Do not take it swimming. If it happens to drop in water, do not let it stay submerged for a long time. At the same time, resist the temptation to use your phone underwater.

Protection from theft and loss

You can lose your phone in different circumstances. With Apple Care+ Theft and Loss Protection, you do not need to worry about these anymore. It will cost you $249, but if you ever lose your iPhone XR, or if it is stolen, you can get a replacement. The good thing about this plan is that you can break it down in manageable installments.

Message Previews on your Lock Screen

How do you want to access your messages? Previews are a good thing. They help you brush through messages without having to lose time reading all of them. By default, your iPhone XR does not show message previews until you scan your face with Face ID. In terms of privacy, this is an awesome feature.

However, some people who need instant access to message previews feel this is too much. For those who prefer the screen waking up irrespective of the angle to access the notifications, using Face ID to preview messages can be a bother. You can disable this easily. Navigate to Settings, then Notifications, and select Show Previews, then choose Always.

Chapter 16: Software at a Glance

The iPhone XR comes with the iOS 12 on it and the software is a part of the iOS 12 bundle. We will run through it so that you know what to expect from an iPhone XR with respect to pre-loaded software.

The iPhone XR coupled with the iOS 12 has a new gesture system. We have already discussed the gesture system in detail in the chapter "First Things First."

Also, note that the iPhone XR does not come with 3D touch like its more expensive siblings, and therefore, the way you can experience a bit of it on the iPhone XR is by simply tapping and holding the screen. This keeps the iPhone XR far behind in the race from its siblings as 3D touch is only used when performing quick actions on the icons and these actions are swifter when you do the tap and hold action.

Let's take a ride through all the apps that come on the iPhone XR as a part of the iOS 12 bundle.

Facetime

Facetime is a proprietary application that was developed by Apple for video communication. Any iOS device equipped with a front facing camera and iOS version 10.6.6 or above supports Facetime. Apple also has an audio version of Facetime called Facetime Audio, which is supported by any Apple device running iOS 7 or higher. Facetime was introduced as a free app in iOS and MacOS from the Mac OS X Lion release.

Photo

All the pictures that you click with your iPhone and iPad are accessible through the Photos app. The app has evolved over the years and now supports editing and sharing features.

Mail

Mail, previously known as Apple mail, is the Email client that is available on Apple devices. It evolved from NeXTMail, which was developed by NeXT originally as a part of the NeXTSTEP OS.

You can configure an email account on mail using popular protocols such as SMTP, POP, and IMAP.

Mail app also supports pre-loaded configurations of popular Email providers such as Google, Yahoo, Hotmail, AOL, etc.

Clock

The clock app lets you set the time of your device. In addition to this, it also supports World time in case you have friends and family in different time zones.

Maps

Apple Maps is an application that is widely

used by the traveling community while touring the world. It also comes handy on a daily routine basis for your commute between work and home as it helps you understand real-time traffic.

Weather

Apple Weather lets to pull weather details from the Apple database for any city, country, or region in the world.

Calendar

The calendar app lets you add entries to the calendar for any upcoming events and let's you plan out your day.

Notes

Notes is a simple app which lets you keep adding notes every now and then you come across something that you wish to jot down for a quick glance later.

Reminders

Reminders app lets you set up appointment reminders or any other reminder, which would show up as a prompt at the time that you have set it for.

Apple News

Why buy a newspaper when you have Apple News? The app gives you access to all the leading newspapers and numerous magazines online. You also get the option to go through past issues of a newspaper or magazine. Additionally, you can also download a magazine to be kept for reading at a later time.

Stocks

If you are a person who invests in the stock market, then stocks is the app you need. You can follow all the daily ups and downs in the stock market. You also get to customize a ticker such that it focuses on the companies that interest you. Business news from all top publications in the world is also included as a part of the stock app.

iTunes Store

It is the hub to listen to all kinds of music, videos, etc. The app adapts to your choices and suggests to you the kind of music you would like.

App Store

App Store is your one-stop destination for all the applications available for your iPhone. These include applications by Apple itself as well as new applications developed by 3rd party Apple application developers.

Books

You can access all the popular books available in the world and purchase them off the Apple Books app.

Home Kit

The Apple Home Kit app basically lets you connect to all Apple supported home devices such as lights, music systems, locks, etc.

Wallet

Apple Wallet is an alternative to carrying your physical credit cards with you everywhere. You can use your wallet to make payments at a number of merchants around the world.

Podcasts

If you are a person who loves listening to podcasts, the podcasts app will let you access all the popular podcasts from around the world at the tap of your finger.

Find My iPhone

Works with your GPS on your Apple phone to help you locate your iPhone in case you end up losing it or misplacing it.

Contacts

The Contacts app is where all your contact details are stored.

Files

The Files App provides you with a File Manager to perform actions on all the files available on your storage in your iPhone. You can move files from one folder to another and organize it in any way you wish.

Watch

The Apple watch on your iPhone lets you customize faces for your watch, configure notifications and settings, install apps on your physical watch, etc.

Voice Memos

Record audio clips on your iPhone and then edit it or share it. After you create a voice memo, you can easily replace a part of it, trim it or even delete a part of it.

Compass

The Compass is a handy app for the traveler in you. It shows you the direction to which your iPhone is pointing, the elevation, and your current location.

Measure

Through the integration of augmented reality, the measure app turns your iPhone into a measuring tape. You can measure the size of objects, detect dimensions of objects, and also save a picture of the measurement to be referred to later.

Calculator

A simple app to perform all the basic mathematical calculations.

Clips

The Clips app lets you create and share video clips by adding simple edits like text, graphics and more to them.

iMovie

iMovie is an application provided by Apple to edit videos. It was released in 1999 originally on Mac OS 8. Once a paid application, iMovie is now offered free of cost on the latest Apple devices.

iTunes U

The app was developed keeping students in mind. The iTunes U app lets you organize homework seamlessly and deliver assignments, lessons, and stay connected with your peers.

Apple TV

The Apple TV app lets you maintain your watchlist with your iPad, iPhone, and your

Apple TV. The Apple TV app was initially only available in the USA but is now available in the UK as well.

Safari

The Safari app is the web browser provided on Apple device, which lets you surf the World Wide Web through a smooth experience.

Phone

The phone app is used to make phone calls to contacts in your iPhone.

Messages

The Messages app is used to send messages using the SMS protocol.

Music

Apple Music is the music player app on your iPhone. It lets you add songs, create playlists, and even suggests songs based on your listening history. This is a subscription-based service.

Sheets

Sheets is Apple's alternative for Google Sheets and Microsoft Excel. If you are a person who likes to work on their worksheets while on the go, the Sheets app will make your life easy.

Pages

Pages is again Apple's alternative to Google Docs and Microsoft Word. It lets you create documents while on the go. It is particularly useful for writers and editors who like to note down things as and when they make a way to their mind.

Keynote

Keynote is Apple's alternative for Google Slides and Microsoft PowerPoint. It lets you create beautiful presentations on the go and is widely used by corporate professionals.

GarageBand

Apple provides a fully equipped virtual studio for creating music. This comes packed with a full-fledged sound library, which includes presets for the guitar and voice, instruments, and a variety of choices for drummers and percussionists. GarageBand has made it very easy to compose, edit, and share new musical compositions with everyone.

Conclusion

The iPhone XR's performance is at par with the iPhone XS series, which means you will be getting a top-notch experience.

The battery life is better than the iPhone XS series and this gives an advantage to the gamer's community as the GPU benefits highly from this and gives a better gaming experience compared to the iPhone XS and XS Max.

What makes the iPhone XR stand out? Even though it made headlines as one of the most affordable iPhones yet, you are still getting some fantastic features. You are getting a phone that is larger than an iPhone X and still offers the same unrivaled user experience. Apple decided to maintain the TrueDepth camera on the iPhone XR, having made a cameo on the iPhone X in 2017.

That aside, the Home button goes away, and so does the Touch ID. In place of the Home button and Touch ID, Apple is introducing TrueDepth camera and Face ID. Without a Home button, you must now swipe on the display from the bottom to get you back to the Home screen, a feature that was introduced with the iPhone X.

In terms of the design, a lot of things about the iPhone XR are a build off the back of iPhone X and iPhone XS. Looking back to the earlier designs, the new iPhone XR also has a similar glass and metal modern design concept which features curves around all corners. At the top, it also has a notch like the predecessors. What Apple has done with the iPhone XR is to continue in the reinvention that was aimed at marking a launch in the next frontier, the future 10 years of the iPhone.

There are notable differences between the iPhone XR and the predecessors. A quick glance will reveal the bezels have been made thicker around the display area. The screen to casing ratio has reduced to give users a complete full-screen effect when using the iPhone XR. However, these are differences that you would barely notice if you were not holding the iPhone XR and a close comparison hand to hand. If you take the comparison further to an iPhone 8, you will notice wholesale differences.

Given the features available on the iPhone XR, who would be the ideal target for it? Well, in case you have an iPhone 8 or any of the older iPhones, you might want to consider getting an iPhone XR.

We finally find ourselves coming to the final paragraph of this little book on the iPhone XR. It is clear that when the iPhone XS series was out, we all agreed that the price being asked by Apple is a tad too much. But with the release of the iPhone XR, Apple has finally played a masterstroke in the smartphone market.

In the end, the final and big question is if the iPhone XR is value for your money with everything that it has to offer and a few things that it lacks in comparison to its more expensive siblings. Well as for the cost, it is definitely the most worthy iPhone that has ever come to the market. The point to be noted is that Apple has not compromised on technology to make the iPhone XR affordable as it is equipped with the latest A12 Bionic processor. All this kept in mind, the iPhone XR definitely provides better value in comparison to the iPhone XS alternatives.

BOOK 3
iPhone XS – XS MAX
The Handy Guide

Introduction

The iPhone is a product that is manufactured and distributed by the multinational technology corpora-tion, Apple, Inc. This company was founded by Steve Jobs, the company's chairman and

CEO, the personal computing pioneer Steve "Woz" Wozniak, and their administrative overseer Ronald Wayne, who ended up selling his 10% share in this new company for a total of $800 USD. Only a year later, he also accepted another $1500 USD to forfeit any potential claims to the newly incorporated entity in the future, for only$2300 USD in total. These men brought the company to life in 1976 in order to sell Wozniak's new personal computer, the Apple I. Later on, they began to design, produce, and sell various electronic products and online services in the global market.

These electronics include the iOS line of devices such as iPod portable media player, iPhone smartphones, and iPad tablet computers. They also sold other products, like the Macintosh personal computer, which utilized the Mac Operating System designed by Apple, the Apple TV, and the HomePod smart speaker.

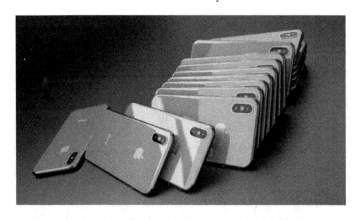

Apple's impressive list of online services consists of useful tools such as the iCloud, iTunes, Apple Music, the iOS App Store, and the Mac App Store. They also provide many more useful products, such as the operating systems MacOS, iOS, and WatchOS, iLife creativity, the web browser Safari, Xcode, Final Cut Pro, and Logic Pro.

Apple was one of the largest earning firms during the fiscal year of 2017 and owned up to $229 billion at the time. They were the third largest seller on a global level, based on the sales of iOS devices alone. Apple maintains and manages around 504 retail stores in 24 major countries, and has the honor of being the employer of 123,000 workers as of 2018. With all of this in mind, it isn't at all surprising that the company is valued at around $1 trillion and has managed to become such a large name in and outside of its industry. The business community, of course, had had quite a large handful of significant comments about the company's carbon footprint, anti-competitive behavior, questionable labor practices, and the actual origin of their raw materials. Apple has, of course, managed to push past these difficulties, though. They have worked hard to gain the trust of their customers and believe very strongly in the concept of brand loyalty.

Over 1 billion individual devices from Apple are being used and adored around the world, and with the interconnectedness and cross-functionality across Apple's various products, this number is constantly increasing at alarming rates.

In an interview from March 2014, the designer of Apple, Inc. referred to the iPhone as "the epitome of high-quality product development". According to him, iPhones are comparatively more expensive than devices from other brands due to the extensive effort and the resources that are utilized in their making. When the company began to manufacture the iPhone, active decisions were made in order to keep their design and properties separate and unique from similar, competing models. Now, there have been several models launched, each with an increased and improved sense of uniqueness and quality, and all of which have seemed to take the world by storm. Recently, Apple Inc.

Has released new versions of the iPhone with even more unique features and higher levels of power and precision. These are the successors to the iPhone X, referred to as the iPhone XS, its larger, upgraded edition called the iPhone XS Max, and the slightly simpler model, which has been named the iPhone XR.

This book intends to illuminate the features of these new devices and their operating system, iOS 12, in great detail. It will include their specifications, pros and cons, tips and tricks to help you use them to their best and fullest capacity, and a clear and differential analysis of the latest products in comparison to their ancestors. By the end, you should possess all of the tools necessary to do so and properly utilize all of the applications and other features available to you on your new iPhone XS, XS Max, or XR.

Chapter 1: Main iPhone Features

The iPhone is special because it seems to have its own completely separate market from similar devices. This is because of the many useful and unique features available exclusively on iPhones. Listed below are all of the Primary features of the iPhone and brief guides on how to use them properly and to their full extent.

Phone:

The first feature will, of course, be the phone function itself. It contains innovative features, like the visual voicemail, which will display voicemails as text to be read, as opposed to the audio format which needs to be listened to. The Phone application will allow you to make calls and view your voicemails. The Phone application's features will be listed below;

- Keypad: Lets you dial numbers manually to call or add to contacts.

- Recents: Lists your recent calls and allows you to redial.

- Contacts: Lists all of your saved contacts and lets you add new ones.

- Favorites: Lists your favorited contacts for easier access.

- Voicemail: Allows you to listen to view and listen to voicemails. Visual Voicemail is an option, as well.

Multi-touch Screen:

While the older iPhone models had a 3.5-inch display, the new iPhone X and XS have a 5.8-inch OLED with a "super retina" display that has a higher pixel count and an impressive upgrade in its dynamic range over the previous models, with an astonishing 60% increase. The multi-touch screen, of course, incorporates a new "Multi-touch" technology. This new feature enables the utilization of multiple points of contact to perform new and useful functions on the touch screen that weren't possible before.

Some of the most discussed features of the iPhone are due to the multi-touch capabilities of the new devices, such as the ability to double tap on the device's screen in order to enlarge the image by zooming in, or by "pinching", which can be done by placing two fingers on the screen and moving them closer together or further apart on the screen in order to zoom in and out of a photograph or webpage. They also have a "3D Touch", which allows you to use varying degrees of pressure and sensitivity when touching the screen in order to see content previews, actions, and contextual menus.

This setting can be enabled in the "General settings" menu, under "accessibility", and then "3D Touch".

Web Browsing:

iPhones offer a complete and comprehensive browsing experience for their users. Unlike Android phones that use dumbed-down, overly-simplistic "mobile" versions of websites, the iPhone's browsers provide a better and more full interface, which is more akin to a traditional "desktop" browser.

Email:

iPhones, much like all smartphones, consist of a robust email experience that can conveniently sync to corporate email servers running Exchange. They contain all of the standard email features that are offered by your carrier, and can even use multiple accounts. These accounts can be managed in the device's "Passwords & Accounts" settings.

Calendar:

In addition to functioning as a phone, the iPhone has the ability to manage your personal information with the help of incredibly handy features such as the address book, weather updates, stock management, and the calendar. The calendar can, of course, be accessed and managed via the "Calendar" application. Through it, you can schedule events and appointments for any point in the future. This is a great way to stay organized and minimize confusion in daily life.

Clock:

The "Clock" application is also useful for scheduling and, obviously, keeping track of time. There are several functions within the application that can be useful for many day-to-day tasks:

- World Clock: Can keep track of multiple timezones, in case you travel or frequently interact with people in or from other timezones.

- Alarm: Another good way to maintain a proper schedule. You can set alarms for certain times, and manage those alarms here.

- Bedtime: If you stick to a consistent sleep schedule, or want to do so, the bedtime function can help you. You can set specific times during which your iPhone will track your sleep patterns. It can also be programmed with "Do Not Disturb", or to have an alarm set when you wish to wake up.

- Stopwatch: The stopwatch will function as a stopwatch. It has stop, start, lap, and reset functions, for timing the amount of time certain tasks take.

- Timer: Exactly like a timer, this function will count down from a set time. You can start, stop, and reset the timer as well.

Audio/Video Playback:

The size of the various models of iOS devices, such as the iPod and iPhone also changed over time. What has been a reliable constant, however, is the exceptional quality of these devices' hardware, which had made the experience of both audio and video based content consumption all the more mesmerizing. You can use services such as the iTunes store or YouTube to easily find media, and consume it in stunning quality.

Cameras:

One of the more major changes made in recent iPhone models, such as the XS, XS Max, and XR are the cameras. While the rear-facing camera still shoots in higher resolution than the front one, these models have enclosed two cameras on each side, as opposed to only one. This allows for depth perception, which produces even higher-quality photos and videos, in addition to the camera's other features and uses like specialized editing, 3D photos, FaceTime, and Animoji.

Applications:

Apple has its own marketplace for applications that can be used for just about anything that Apple devices can be used for, from tools like flashlights, compasses, and gyroscopes to games like Fruit Ninja, Flappy Bird, and Angry Birds. Some of these applications can require payment to be used, but often there are free versions with ads embedded to help the developers support themselves if they choose to release these free applications. This marketplace is called the Apple App Store, and its third-party programs help to add even more versatility and value to these already incredibly flexible devices. Once an Application is installed, it will be placed on the home screen for easy access.

Home Screen:

The iPhone has a very user-friendly interface that allows its users to rearrange their application icons to their preference. The user can create folders and group icons accordingly, or leave applications outside on the home screen if they so choose. This is where new applications downloaded from the App Store will go by default. You can press and hold on an icon to bring up options for that application, if you want to uninstall or move it.

Home Button:

The home button is placed at the bottom center of the phone and is used to wake the phone and open the App Switcher, which allows you to view open applications and close them, if you choose. In recent models of the iPhone, this button has been removed. The home button is now a part of the multi-touch screen as a digital button on the bottom of your iPhone XS, XS Max, or XR's display.

Hold Button:

The "Hold Button" can be located on the right side of your device, toward the top of the screen. It is a small, oblong button that you can feel by sliding your finger along the device's side. The primary function of this button, which you will end up using the most, is to lock and unlock the screen and put the device to sleep or wake it up. It is also used to restart the phone and power it down completely. This can be done by holding it for several seconds until a "power off" slider appears on the device's display.

Volume Buttons:

The device's volume control buttons can be located on the device's left side, across from the hold button. There are two volume buttons, one up and one down. They are used to control the device's volume settings, including the ringer, videos, and music players.

Ringer Switch:

Located directly over the volume buttons, near the top of your device on the left side, is a small, oblong switch. This switch will allow the user to place their device in "silent mode" in order to prevent their device from ringing audibly when it receives calls. If this switch is in the red position, this means it is on, and your device won't ring audibly. To turn it off, simply flip the switch again.

Dock Connector:

The more recent iPhone models have added wireless charging as a new feature. This capability is present in the XS and XS Max iPhone models, but is unfortunately absent in the XR. There is, however, still a dock port for lightning connectors provided on the bottom side of the device. This is provided for the purpose of charging, with the lightning cable. It can also be used for data transfer, and can be plugged into a computer to sync with iTunes and move files from one device to the other. There are also many accessories, such as headphones, that can be used through this port as well.

Sync:

As soon as the iPhone is activated for the first time, the user is instructed to input their details to the device. This includes your Apple ID, which enables the phone to sync personal data such as the calendar and contacts, if they were previously backed up to the iCloud. It is also recommended that users periodically back up their device with iTunes, as well. These methods can be helpful in preventing data loss in the case of accidental damage or if the device has been lost or stolen. This can be done over the iCloud from the settings, under [Your Name], in the "iCloud" submenu. If you manually back up your device to the iCloud, however, it will not automatically back up as scheduled for 24 hours afterward. This can be important to note if you have automatic backups scheduled.

Reset and Restore:

The iTunes application can also be used to reset your iPhone to its factory settings and to restore content from a previous backup when issues arise that cause your device to become unusable, and the only way to rectify these issues is to erase the device's contents. This can happen if the device is sent to recovery mode. If your device becomes unusable, you might have to put it into recovery mode in order to restore it from an iTunes backup. This can be done by pressing the up volume button, then the down button, and then pressing the lock button and holding it until your device displays the apple logo on its screen. You will then be able to plug your device into your windows or Mac computer with iTunes and restore it from an old backup by following the prompts provided from the iTunes program.

Chapter 2: Novelties and Unique Features

Super Retina Display:

The new iPhone models consist of a 5.8-inch OLED screen display, similar to iPhone X. They also, however, contain an upgraded component in the screen, which is referred to as the "Super Retina Display". This new display style has a much improved dynamic range over the previous model. It is able to pack more pixels as well, and overall carries a much higher resolution, for smoother images and a brighter display. The new iPhone's Super Retina Display sets the record for the largest display of its type, containing approximately 3.3 million pixels.

Face Recognition:

A product of the dual-camera setup's depth perception, face recognition is one of the amazing and novel features that make the iPhone so secure. This feature allows a user to use their face to unlock their device by placing their face in front of the cameras.

Although this feature is also present in some newer Samsung models, the iPhone's facial recognition technology is unique in that it used the 3D capabilities of the dual cameras in order to get a more accurate image of the user's face. This allows for a more accurate reading, which not only makes it easier for the user to use, but also improves the overall security of the device. Apple takes great pride in their many advanced security features and challenges that this facial recognition lock cannot be breached even by professionally-made face masks.

Animoji:

As all companies are developing their own versions of emojis, Apple has decided to take that concept a step further with emojis that are able to work in cooperation with facial recognition software in a fun and immersive way. The facial recognition software captures your image and matches it with the emoji that you are using in order to animate the image and allow you even more creativity than ever. These "animated emojis" are cleverly referred to as "Animoji". If you record a short clip of your face making an expression, gesturing your head, or talking, the animoji will mimic those actions with surprising precision and allow you to record these actions with the animoji filter to send to whoever you may wish to send them to.

Wireless Charging:

The iPhone 8, the 8 Plus, and the iPhone X were the first iPhone models that were designed and manufactured with wireless charging capabilities. The method of wireless charging chosen by Apple can be slow at times, but with newer, more recent models, the wireless charging capabilities have seen significant improvement which will only grow more with time and progress. While the iPhone XS and XS Max are capable of charging wirelessly, the iPhone XR does not possess this incredibly useful and convenient technology.

A12 Bionic Processor:

The A12 Bionic processor in the new iPhone is one of the fastest chips on the planet. This 7 nanometer-wide chip contains 6.7 billion transistors. It also possesses and an 8- core devoted engine with machine learning capabilities to evaluate data sent from a neural network in order for it to decide if the processes should be carried out through that neural engine or not. The A12 Bionic processor uses less energy and can perform 5 trillion operations per second, giving it the ability to open apps 30 times faster than previous iPhones

Cameras:

iPhones have always had amazing quality in their cameras, especially compared to competing devices. With wide-angle camera lens with a resolution of 12 megapixels, and another secondary camera for things like capturing 3D images and registering depth perception, the new iPhone models' cameras offer massive upgrades compared to the ones featured in older devices, such as the iPhone 7 Plus, the first model to feature a telescoping lens. You can also see noticeably smoother photos and videos, better low- light photograph quality, and more. Additionally, with the newer "True

Depth" camera in the front-side, you will be able to take better portrait-style photos, thanks to a feature that was also new to the 7 Plus, which can create a "Bokeh" effect with improved focusing technology that blurs the background slightly in order to highlight the foreground more, in order to help create a more professional-looking photo. You can also adjust the photo depth with the depth slider. The XS and XS Max can both still support a vertical configuration camera with improved tone LED flash accompanied by an advanced flicker system in its 12-megapixel telephoto lens camera. The front-facing camera has 2 times faster sensors with improved red-eye reduction, along with detailed segmentation to further boost the quality of all of your photos and videos.

Smart HDR:

In the XS model, a smart HDRA is powered by the same A12 chip that allows the phone's image signal processor and neural engine to chain multiple pictures into one by using techniques like zero shutter lag and highlight, and result in better picture quality. The camera is now also able to take improved photos, make videos with greater highlight structure in low-light conditions.

Apple Bookstore:

The Apple Bookstore is handy when looking for new books to read, or old ones you liked. It considers information such as the authors, genres, and topics in order to make it easier than ever to find interesting reading material. Within the application, you can easily shuffle between books you may be reading quickly, without needing to close one and open the other manually. You can also add books to your wishlist to help you keep track of the ones you want to read next, and purchase them with ease.

Apple Music:

Apple Music is a fun and efficient way of

listening to the music you like. The iPhone provides the Apple Music application, which helps you to personalize your music according to your own taste. You can find specific songs by searching by the song title, artist, album, or even the lyrics. Apple Music will also recommend your top songs from daily charts and your own history.

Apple News:

For those who like to stay up-to-date with current events, iOS offers the "Apple News" application, which can help you keep track of events as they occur. Apple News can suggest articles based on your own interests, as well, to help you stay informed regarding the topics that interest you. With Apple News, it has become easier than ever to stay informed and find material relevant to specific topics that interest you.

Chapter 3: Differences Between iPhone Models

As the past decade has gone by, Apple has continuously introduced newer iPhone models that are each better and more advanced than the last one. This chapter will be taking you through the journey of iPhone models up to the current models that have allowed Apple to take its place as one of the world's most high-tech and successful mobile phone manufacturers.

The iPhone 3G didn't have 3G data or GPS, both of which were introduced later on the following year with a second version which also had a better body. Its current battery was 1150 mA with a Voltage of 3.7 V, and it consisted of Bluetooth 2.0 EDR with a rear camera of 1.9 megapixels, surely nowhere near the latest iPhone models. Its core design was ARM1176 x 1 with a CPU speed of 412 MHz and it had 128 MB RAM, whereas the new latest RAM ranges to 525 GB. In another year, Apple released the iPhone 3GS where S meant "speed." Its battery was better as compared to the previous iPhone with 1219mA. It has a 3.1 rear camera. The core design of this phone was ARM Cortex-A8 x 1 with a CPU speed of 620 MHz and 256 MB of RAM.

After this came the iPhone 4 which looked better than all the previous phones. The front camera was first introduced in the iPhone 4, and took its popularity to a whole new level. It had a better battery of 1419mA and rear camera of 5.2 megapixels, whereas the front camera was 0.3 megapixels. Its core design was ARM Cortex-A8 x 1 with a CPU

Speed of 800 MHz but their RAM and storage space was similar to the previous iPhones. The iPhone 4s didn't have many changes in comparison to its predecessor. One new feature that the iPhone 4s introduced was the entry of Siri and a high-resolution camera, which was able to record play a 1080pHD videos.

The iPhone 5 came with bigger screen displays due to consumer demand. These phones were a quarter inch taller than their predecessors. The width was kept similar. This phone was not user-friendly because of its length, and could not support easy usage with a hand, but the iPhone 5 was one of the first iPhones to support LTE (wireless internet communication technology). It was also one of the first phones to use the new lightning port for charging and data transfer that had been developed by Apple, as opposed to their older, wider 30-pin connectors that were present in previous versions of the iPhone and iPod. It had a 1GB RAM and a 64GB storage space with an 8 megapixels rear camera and a 1.2 megapixels front camera. In the iPhone 5S, the main change was the introduction of the Touch ID fingerprint scanner. Previously, this feature was used only for App Stores and authentic downloads but, in later iPhones, new security additions have been made, such as face recognition. They had introduced the color gold for the first time through this iPhone. The iPhone 5c was comparatively cheaper than the 5S and was the only model since the iPhone 3GS to have a plastic body and a selection of different colors. At $499, it was $200 cheaper than iPhone 5S but was still considered expensive in comparison to other mid-level smartphones. In short, Apple failed to produce a budget friendly smartphone in 2015.

The iPhone 6 and 6 Plus had a far better design than the awkwardly elongated design of their predecessor. Both models were very similar in features. The significant external difference being that of screen size with the 6 Plus consisting of a larger screen. The only internal difference was the presence of an optical image stabilizer in the iPhone 6 Plus that allowed the Apps to be displayed in landscape mode in larger devices. These were also the first Apple phones to feature the much celebrated Apple Pay. After this came the famous iPhone 6S which introduced a new feature called "3D Touch." Also known as 'pressure touch' users could, for the first time, carry out different tasks by pressing the screen harder. The iPhone 6S was the first model to be launched in rose gold; the most popular skin of all time. The iPhone SE, on the other hand, is one of the smallest phones that Apple developed. It is an attempt for a budget-friendly smartphone for emerging markets. It has the exterior of iPhone 5S i.e. a plastic body and small screen size of just 4 inches but comes with all the powerful features of the iPhone 6S.

With the launch of iPhone 7 and 7 Plus, Apple again launched two models at the same time with different screen sizes and price points. The iPhone 7 and 7 Plus were the first iPhones to come without a headphone jack. They were also the first iPhones that did not have a physical home button and also the first iPhones that were waterproof. Unlike the iPhone 7, the iPhone 7 Plus consisted of a double-rear camera which could measure depth, resulting in quite impressive portrait shots.

Apple released the new iPhone 8 and 8 Plus on September 12, 2017. These new models were presented as the most recent in the line of upgrades to Apple's iOS Devices. They possessed better, more efficient processors and many other features designed to maximize the iPhone's potential and effectiveness. The iPhone 8 had upgraded camera hardware and better displays with improved resolution as well, for even higher-quality visual content creation and consumption. Of course, they also possessed the new wireless charging technology that Apple had developed, which was a somewhat controversial topic at the time but ultimately served to improve the overall quality of iPhone use and made them easier and more enjoyable to use. Apple had also revealed the iPhone X, which altered the iPhone's hardware even further. The iPhone X introduced a new feature designed to streamline the use of Apple's devices moving forward, by removing the home button that was present in previous models and replaced them with the new digital home indicator bar. They also added new gesture technology, wireless charging capabilities, and facial recognition software.

Apple finally introduced the successors to the iPhone X on September 12, 2018. These new models were referred to as the iPhone XS, XS Max, and XR. The iPhone XS and XS Max featured new "Super Retina" displays as well as a new and improved dual-camera system. This new camera technology allowed for, as with many of the iPhone's previous models, higher-quality photos and videos. Other features include the first chip to be included in a mobile computing device of seven nanometers and another new feature in the A12 Bionic chip, with access to a new neural engine. It was also given faster and more accurate FaceID features, improved stereo sound output range, and the introduction of the iPhone's new Dual SIM capabilities, which allowed for two SIM cards within a single device. The iPhone XR comes with the most impressive smartphone LCD to date, containing a new 6.1-inch Liquid Retina display, the new A12 Bionic chip, and the True Depth dual-camera system that allows for three-dimensional images and the capacity for depth perception for higher-quality photos and videos.

Chapter 4: iPhone XS

The newer model of iPhone , the iPhone XS, is slightly smaller than its predecessor, the iPhone X. It does, however, have many new features and upgrades over the older model that will be described in this chapter.

Price per Capacity:

The price of this iPhone depends on its capacity. It's $999 for the 64GB, $1,149 for the 256GB or $1,349 for the 512GB.

Colors:

The iPhone XS is available in a stainless-steel body that comes in three colors: space grey, gold, and silver.

Screen/Display:

The iPhone XS possesses a decently-sized diagonal 5.8 inches in a 458 pixel-per-inch OLED "Super Retina" HDR display, whereas the iPhone 8 Plus only had a total screen size of 5.5 inches. The iPhone XS does have slightly less total volume in its screen, however, as it is also slightly thinner as well.

Height:

The iPhone XS has a height of 5.65 inches, or 143.6 mm.

Weight:

It is 6.24 ounces (177 grams) heavy.

Depth:

The depth of iPhone XS is 0.30-inch (7.7 mm).

Width:

The width of iPhone XS is 2.79-inches (70.9 mm).

Splash Water and Dust Resistant:

The iPhone XS is resistant to both water and dust. It is waterproof and has been estimated to be able to last for approximately 30 minutes at a depth of up to 2 meters when fully submerged in water.

Bionic Chip:

This new chip contains artificial intelligence software that reaches entirely new tiers of efficiency and excellence. The A12 Bionic Chip, paired with a next-generation neural engine, to deliver impressive results. For example, it provides powerful real-time machine learning that produces amazing results for gaming, photos, augmented reality, etc. This chip has increased the speed of functions by 15% as compared to the A11 Bionic chip. It also allows the device an additional 50% higher efficient battery consumption rate over the a11 model. The A12 Bionic chip delivers a 50% faster graphics performance. Apple designed this new neural engine to allow its devices to learn from its users based on their patterns and preferences in order to make accurate predictions for things like text corrections and product advertisements that might interest their users based on this information. All of this new technology helps to make the iPhone XS, XS Max, and XR that much more capable and efficient to maximize their users' satisfaction.

Camera:

It consists of Smart HDR that encapsulates multiple technologies inside it. It encompasses faster sensors, an enhanced ISP, and advanced algorithms. Smart HDR is used to enhance the quality of photos through better highlight and shadow. The new iPhones have even more effective technology that allow for better effects, like the Bokeh, or background blur effect, for better quality portrait Photos. The camera produces a new "True Depth" depth map to keep the background blurred while the user is in focus helping to deliver enhanced portrait mode photos. This new iPhone's camera's sensors use new rendering technology and allow more thorough light sensors within the camera's hardware in order to help improve the quality of any photos you might take in low light conditions, as well as the photos you take in normal conditions as well. These new sensors combine with a new feature that allows for effectively no shutter-lag to erase any motion-blur in your photos and create more prominent highlights and detailed shadows as well. The iPhone XS can also record videos with amazing quality with the help of its new low light filters at a consistent rate of 30 frames per second, and can even maintain dual-channel audio recording and playback.

Facial Landmarking:

Once a face is detected, facial landmarking allows the iPhone camera to adjust the portrait lightning as per the subject in focus.

Mapping the Depth:

The iPhone has the ability to keep the subject and the background separate due to the advanced neural engine combined with advanced depth engine of ISP.

Moreover, Portrait mode captures depth information that lets you adjust the depth of field and add creative Portrait Lighting effects. It consists of twin 12-megapixel rear- facing cameras with wide angle lenses. In addition, it has a 7MP True Depth front camera with a $f/2.2$ wide-angle lens.

Power and Battery:

The battery of iPhone XS Lasts up to 30 minutes longer than the iPhone X. It has a built-in rechargeable lithium-ion battery inside it. It is supported by wireless charging (works with Qi chargers), and it can also be charged through a USB to a computer system or power adapter.

Talk Time (Wireless):

After one full charge, the talk time can last up to 20 hours.

Internet Use:

It can support up to 12 hours of continuous internet use from a full charge.

Video Playback (Wireless):

The user can easily play videos up to 14 hours after a full charge.

Audio Playback (Wireless):

It provides the facility of up to 60 hours of audio playback after a full charge.

Fast-Charge Capable:

It takes the iPhone XS, only 30 minutes to charge 50%.

Sensors:

The iPhone XS consists of three-axis gyro, Accelerometer, Proximity sensor, Ambient light sensor, and Barometer.

SIM Card:

It has a Dual SIM (nano-SIM and eSIM) which is not compatible with existing micro-SIM cards

Connector:

It consists of a Lightning charging port.

Audio Calling:

You can initiate audio calls over WiFi or cellular to any FaceTime audio-enabled device.

Secure Authentication:

It uses Face identification for a higher level of personal security which is improved by the True Depth camera's 3d image capture capabilities for depth perception and more accurate readings of your face for security purposes.

Chapter 5: iPhone XS Max

If you are into watching movies, taking photos, recording videos, or doing anything involving the screen, then the iPhone XS Max is the one for you. This chapter will be similar to the last, and will list details and features of the iPhone XS Max.

Price per Capacity:

Obviously, the iPhone XS Max is a little

different than the XS. It is a little bit larger and beefier, and as such, the prices are also a bit higher. The price of this iPhone depends on the capacity, though, as with the standard XS model. The XS Max is a very simple and clean $100 increase in price over the XS, with prices listed at $1099 for the 64GB, $1,249 for the 256GB, and an impressive $1,449 for the 512GB.

Colors:

The iPhone XS is available in a stainless-steel body that comes in three colors, just as with the iPhone XS. These color options are space grey, gold, and stainless steel silver.

Screen/Display:

With an even more astonishing 19.5:9 aspect ratio and a 6.5-inch diagonal True Tone "Super Retina" 458 pixels-per-inch display and an objective screen resolution of 2688 x 1242 pixels, the iPhone XS steps it up just a bit with the same type of display as the XS, but slightly larger overall.

Height:

The iPhone XS Max has a height of 6.2 inches, or 157.5 mm.

Depth:

The depth of iPhone XS Max is the same as the standard XS, at 0.30-inch (7.7 mm).

Width:

The width of iPhone XS Max is 3.05-inches (77.4).

Weight:

The iPhone XS Max weighs in at 7.34 ounces, or 208 grams.

Splash Water and Dust Resistant:

The iPhone XS Max, just like the XS, resistant to both water and dust. It is waterproof and has been estimated to be able to last for approximately 30 minutes at a depth of up to 2 meters when fully submerged in water.

Bionic Chip:

This new chip contains artificial intelligence software that reaches entirely new tiers of efficiency and excellence. The A12 Bionic Chip, paired with a next-generation neural engine, to deliver impressive results. For example, it provides powerful real-time machine learning that produces amazing results for gaming, photos, augmented reality, etc. This chip has increased the speed of functions by 15% as compared to the A11 Bionic chip. It also allows the device an additional 50% higher efficient battery consumption rate over the a11 model. The A12 Bionic chip delivers a 50% faster graphics performance. Apple designed this new neural engine to allow its devices to learn from its users based on their patterns and preferences in order to make accurate predictions for things like text corrections and product advertisements that might interest their users based on this information. All of this new technology helps to make the iPhone XS, XS Max, and

XR that much more capable and efficient to maximize their users' satisfaction.

Camera:

It consists of Smart HDR that encapsulates multiple technologies inside it. It encompasses faster sensors, an enhanced ISP, and advanced algorithms. Smart HDR is used to enhance the quality of photos through better highlight and shadow. The new iPhones have even more effective technology that allow for better effects, like the Bokeh, or background blur effect, for better quality portrait Photos. The camera produces a new "True Depth" depth map to keep the background blurred while the user is in focus helping to deliver enhanced portrait mode photos. This new iPhone's camera's sensors use new rendering technology and allow more thorough light sensors within the camera's hardware in order to help improve the quality of any photos you might take in low light conditions, as well as the photos you take in normal conditions as well. These new sensors combine with a new feature that allows for effectively no shutter-lag to erase any motion-blur in your photos and create more prominent highlights and detailed shadows as well. The iPhone XS can also record videos with amazing quality with the help of its new low light filters at a consistent rate of 30 frames per second, and can even maintain dual-channel audio recording and playback.

Facial Landmarking:

Once a face is detected, facial landmarking allows the iPhone camera to adjust the portrait lightning as per the subject in focus.

Mapping the Depth:

The iPhone has the ability to keep the subject and the background separate due to the advanced neural engine combined with advanced depth engine of ISP.

Moreover, Portrait mode captures depth information that lets you adjust the depth of field and add creative Portrait Lighting effects. It consists of twin 12-megapixel rear- facing cameras with wide angle lenses. In addition, it has a 7MP True Depth front camera with a $f/2.2$ wide-angle lens.

Power and Battery:

The battery of iPhone XS Max Lasts up to 90 minutes longer than the iPhone X. It is supported by wireless charging (works with Qi chargers), and it can also be charged through a USB to a computer system or power adapter.

Talk Time (Wireless):

After one full charge, the talk time can last for as long as 25 hours.

Internet Use:

It can handle as many as 13 hours of continuous internet use from a full charge.

Video Playback (Wireless):

The user can easily play videos up to 14 hours after a full charge.

Audio Playback (Wireless):

It provides the facility of up to 60 hours of audio playback after a full charge.

Fast-Charge Capable:

It takes the iPhone XS, only 30 minutes to charge 50%.

Sensors:

The iPhone XS consists of three-axis gyro, Accelerometer, Proximity sensor, Ambient light sensor, and Barometer.

SIM Card:

It has a Dual SIM (nano-SIM and eSIM) which is not compatible with existing micro-SIM cards

Connector:

It consists of a Lightning charging port.

Audio Calling:

You can initiate audio calls over WiFi or cellular to any FaceTime audio-enabled device.

Secure Authentication:

It uses Face identification for a higher level of personal security which is improved by the True Depth camera's 3d image capture capabilities for depth perception and more accurate readings of your face for security purposes.

Chapter 6: Tips and Tricks

There are many ways to utilize the iPhone XS, XS Max, and XR to their maximum efficiency, but some of their shortcuts may not immediately intuitive at a glance. Some of the features of these devices aren't necessarily things that you would think to use if you aren't already familiar with them. This isn't to say, of course, that they can't be useful, though. Several of these shortcuts can be extremely helpful in day-to-day life and will let you streamline your experience with your new device. Listed below are some tips and tricks to help you get the most out of your iPhone XS, XS Max, or XR.

Power Off:

In order to turn off the phone, or make an emergency call with your iPhone XS, hold the side button and one of the volume buttons at the same time, and then drag to turn off the device, use the Medical ID or make an emergency call.

Reset:

Performing a hard reset on the iPhone XS is a little bit more complicated than just turning the device off with the power slider. Luckily, this manual reset method is also fairly simple. You need to press the volume up button on the left side of the device.

Then, press the volume down button directly below. Finally, you will need to press and hold the power button on the right side of the screen for several seconds, until the Apple logo appears on the screen. Once this logo appears, the full reset can take about 20 to 30 seconds.

Emergency Calls:

In order to turn off the phone, or make an emergency call with your iPhone XS, hold the side button and one of the volume buttons at the same time, and then drag to turn off the device, use the Medical ID or make an emergency call.

Medical ID:

In order to turn off the phone, or make an emergency call with your iPhone XS, hold the side button and one of the volume buttons at the same time, and then drag to turn off the device, use the Medical ID or make an emergency call.

Tap to Wake iPhone:

Your device can be set in such a way that it will allow you to tap on the 3-D display in order to wake your phone up. This is a default setting, but you can also enable or disable it manually by going into the Settings App, selecting "General", moving to the "Accessibility" submenu, and tapping "Tap To Wake" to toggle this feature on or off.

Attention-Aware Features:

The iPhone XS can be customized in other ways, as well. You can also activate the "Raise to Wake" setting to allow you to wake up your device without tapping on it or swiping it. This can be done by going to the "Display and Brightness" submenu in your device settings, and toggling on or off the "Raise to Wake" option.

Face ID Lock:

With the addition of iOS 12, the newer models of the iPhone have a strong 3D facial recognition tool for security which is considered more reliable as compared to fingerprint recognition. Just go into the

Settings App, under the "Face ID & Passcode" submenu and follow the instructions. You can also control the apps which use this feature under the "Face ID & Passcode" settings, in "Other Apps".

Home Indicator Bar:

In order to go back to the home screen directly from an open application, you will need to use the new Home Indicator Bar at the bottom of the screen on your iPhone. You simply need to swipe up quickly from the bar on the bottom of the screen, and this action will send you to the device's home screen. If you have multiple pages of application icons on your device, this action will return you to the first page.

App Switcher:

The App Switcher can be incredibly useful in switching between applications and closing ones that aren't being used. In order to get to the App Switcher, you simply need to swipe left or right from the Home Indicator

Bar on the bottom of the screen. Once you do this, all of your open applications will be displayed on the screen. You can scroll among or between applications in order to open a different one, if it is already open, or swipe up or down to close an application as well.

Control Center:

The Control Center lets you change settings on your device quickly, such as brightness, volume, and Bluetooth connectivity. To get to the Control Center, you will need to start from the top of the screen on the right side, and swipe downward. To dismiss it, you can swipe your finger in the opposite direction, from the bottom to the top. This will dismiss panel for this function. The Control Center has many settings that are embedded by default. These settings include various different "cards", which will be listed below:

The first card contains connectivity settings, which can be accessed in a small window in the upper left-hand corner of the Control center:

Airplane Mode: Instantly activate or disable connectivity to and from your iPhone.

Cellular Data: Instantly activate and disable connectivity for applications or services.

Wi-Fi: Activate or disable WiFi connectivity to your device.

Bluetooth: activate or disable Bluetooth connectivity in order to connect to or disconnect from Bluetooth capable devices.

AirDrop: Activate or disable AirDrop to allow you to share media with other Apple products.

Personal Hotspot: Activate or disable your device's personal hotspot, which broadcasts your cell signal as a wireless internet connection point.

You can also find the Audio card in the

control center's top right-hand corner. Press firmly or press and hold to access this card in order to quickly access its full functionality. It can be used to control any audio-based media you may have active, including music, audiobooks, and podcasts. You can tap the radar icon in this window to change the sound source to any compatible and ready audio output device. It will also display individual cards dedicated to any nearby available devices. Simply tap those cards to control that device's audio output as well.

The Control Center also has many settings within it that you can change, and you can even add or remove various features, depending on your preference. To change the Shortcuts available to you on your Control Center screen, you can go to the device's settings menu, and continue on to the "Control Center" submenu. From here, tap on the "Customize" option. From this menu, you can Add features with the + icon, or remove them with the - icon. You can also rearrange these shortcuts with the icons on the right side of each feature that resemble three horizontal lines. The customizable features of the Control Center that can be changed will be listed below:

- Alarm: You can use this card to help you create alarms for yourself.

- Brightness: You can use this card to change the brightness on your device by sliding the bar.

- Calculator: This card pulls up the calculator application, which functions as a standard calculator or a scientific calculator depending on the screen orientation.

- **Do Not Disturb:** this card will let you turn on do not disturb mode. You can set a timeframe for this mode or simply turn it on and deactivate it whenever you choose.

- Do Not Disturb While Driving: This card can be turned on to activate do not disturb mode when you are driving, and will send a quick message to anyone attempting to get in touch with you that you are unavailable.

- Guided Access: this card can restrict which applications or services your device is able to access.

- Low Power Mode: toggling this card will activate low power mode in order to preserve battery life.

- Magnifier: this will activate the camera in order to allow you to use your iPhone as a magnifying glass.

- Scan QR Code: This card will pull up the camera application to scan and open the content within a QR code

- Rotation Lock: This setting will prevent your device from switching its screen orientation.

- **Silent Mode: place your device in silent mode to avoid hearing the** ringer or notification tones.

- Stopwatch: This card will pull up the clock application's stopwatch function.

- Text Size: This card will let you adjust the size of text that appears on the screen.

- Voice Memos: This card will allow you to use your iPhone's microphone to record an audio clip.

- Volume: This card will let you change the volume of auditory output from your device.

Certain cards have even more functionality. You can press deeply or press and hold in order to view more controls for these cards, listed below:

- Accessibility Shortcuts: This card will make it simpler to activate or deactivate accessibility shortcuts.

- Apple TV Remote: This card will make it easier to control any Apple TV related products from your iPhone.

- Camera: This card will open the camera application for easy access to photo and video capturing.

- Flashlight: Activating this card will toggle your iPhone's rear facing LED light to be used as a flashlight with adjustable brightness settings.

- Hearing Aids: This card will allow you to easily pair your iPhone with heading aids for easier accessibility.

- Home: This card lets you easily access the settings for the Home application.

- Night Shift: This card lets you activate the settings for night mode, which filter out the blue light for nighttime consumption.

- Notes: This card will allow you to easily access the note pad application.

- Screen Mirroring: This card allows you to share your screen with available devices.

- Screen Recording: This card will allow you to capture video of your device's display, much like a screenshot image. You can also capture audio with it, if you choose to do so.

- Timer: The timer card will allow you to access the clock application's timer function.

- True Tone: This card will allow you to alter the color and brightness settings of your device's display to best suit your current environment and time of day.

- Wallet: This card will enable you to quickly access your saved payment information for apple pay.

Notification Bar:

Swipe from the left edge of the screen towards the right for the notification bar to appear. This screen will display any notifications from apps available at the time, and allow you to either clear the notification, which will remove it from the list, or tap the notification, which will then open the relevant application for you immediately.

Do Not Disturb:

This is a feature that lets you keep your personal time to yourself without being interrupted by any phone calls or messages. You can easily customize the time period during which you prefer not to be disturbed. After you set the times, the iPhone will automatically go into "Do Not Disturb" mode within those specified timings. When Do Not Disturb is activated, you will see a crescent moon icon on the status bar. You can activate this mode in multiple ways. You can set it from the "Do Not Disturb" submenu in the device settings or from its card in the Control Center.

Low Power Mode:

A very useful tool that can be used to extend the battery life on your device is the "Low Power Mode" setting. You can convert the phone into power saving mode by going into 'Settings", under the "Battery" submenu. This will help you in various ways to use your phone longer and conserve battery life. You can also see the App utilization from the bar above and close Apps that are using more space and battery to maximize battery life.

Screenshot:

Screenshots can be useful for capturing your screen as an image, without having to take a physical photograph of your device. To do this, hold the side button and the top volume button at the same time.

Tap to Top:

When going through long notes and documents, going back at the top can seem like a time-consuming and frustrating hassle. In order to save yourself from that, just tap the very top of your iPhone's screen and it will take you back to the very first page of the document.

Quickly Add Symbols:

In order to help you use your new device to its full functionality, there are many tools within its programming to streamline its use. The keyboard, for example, has a shortcut to add symbols quickly without forcing the user to scroll through multiple specialized keyboards. You can tap and hold certain keys within the device's keyboard in order to pull up various symbols and characters that would otherwise require several steps to use.

Customized Auto-Correct:

The iPhone's operating system, iOS, is quick at guessing what you might want to type next. In order to customize your text patterns and mannerisms, this predictive text feature can be useful. In order to manage this feature, you can go to your device's general settings, scroll down and tap Keyboard. Select Text Replacement and you will see what text replacements you currently have set up.

Rich Formatting:

Rich formatting is a handy trick to make certain parts of your App's texts stand out and be different. Click open a rich formatting App, select the text that you want to edit by tapping it twice and choose the formatting menu.

Speak Selection:

You can have your iPhone XS read out your texts by simply enabling speak selection. To do this, go into 'General Settings' and choose the 'Accessibility' option. Select 'Speak Selection' from there. Once you do this, you will be able to find the option to 'Speak' in your messages by long pressing it.

Saved Information:

In order to save time in filling the same account information again and again, you can make your iPhone memorize the details so when it is time to input the data, your iPhone auto fills the required information. Just go to the device settings and select "Autofill" under the "Safari" submenu.

Customized Message Replies to Missed Calls:

You can easily customize replies and keep them for the calls that you are unable to answer. This is handy when you don't have time to type a message. These messages can be set under the "Phone settings, in the "Respond With Text" Submenu.

Call Reminders:

You can set your iPhone to remind you to make calls at certain times, in case you miss a call or have one scheduled. This can be accomplished from the "Reminders" Application on the home screen. If you are unable to receive a call when it comes in, you can tap the "Remind Me" button to set the reminder for a specific time.

Customize Animoji:

Customized animoji can be set up with the help of the facial recognition tool. The system recognizes your facial expressions in the front camera. Simply pull up the App drawer in the message App, swipe toward the right, and select the animoji icon. This icon will resemble the monkey emoji. Then swipe right until you see the new memoji icon, which will resemble a plus symbol. This allows the user to customize their memoji as they like. After you are finished, tap the "Done" button at the top of the screen to save your memoji and use them in your iMessages.

Video Recording:

You can record videos on your iPhone by using the "Camera" application. This can be accessed from the home screen, or from the control center if you have its card enabled. You can also set the camera to record higher resolution videos by going into the settings, under "Photos & Camera". You can then scroll down and select the "Camera" submenu and tap "Record Video" to change the resolution.

Taking Photos While Recording:

The amazing possibility of taking pictures while shooting a video is what makes shooting fun and easy. In order to take a photo, simply hit the small photo icon that on your device's display, while still continuing to hold the record button for your video. This will decrease the quality of the images, but not to an extreme degree.

YouTube Zoom:

In order to take full advantage of large HD displays, Apple added a feature where you can zoom into the YouTube video to spread them over the landscape display canvas by merely pinching into the screen.

Customized Music Timer:

There is a timer on the Music App in the iPhone XS. You might want to go to sleep while listening to music and, while at it, your phone will be playing songs throughout the night. This can run your battery down, heavily. You can turn on the timer and set the time by which you would like the music to stop. Open the Clock App's timer tab. Select how long you want your timer to last for and then press 'When Timer Ends.' Select 'Stop Playing' from the bottom of the menu. Tap 'start' on the timer and continue listening to the music using the Music App.

The music will automatically stop playing when the timer ends. This technique also works on audio books and other types of media.

Siri Activation:

Activating Siri on the iPhone models of the XS, XS Max, and XR can be somewhat different when compared to their earlier models. This is because of the exclusion of a physical home button. With the new digital home bar, accomplishing simple tasks is now a little bit different, as several of these gestures have had to be remapped to new ones that accommodate this new setup. Luckily, the new commands for these services are just as simple as before. To activate Siri, for example, utilizes the few Face ID, gesture controls, and the hold button on the right side of the iPhone. To activate Siri, you simply need to press and hold the hold button on the right side of the device. After a brief moment, Siri will open and pop up. If Type to Siri is enabled, the device's keyboard will also open, allowing you to type to talk to Siri, as opposed to speaking out loud. You can also, if this feature is enabled, tap the dictation button on your keyboard to speak audibly to communicate with Siri as well. Additionally, you can take this another step further and simply say aloud, "Hey, Siri" in order to activate Siri. This is useful for moments when you may not want to spend time pushing the physical buttons on your phone, as well.

Apple Pay:

Apple Pay is another useful feature that can help to streamline your day-to-day dealings. With it, you can connect your bank account and use your iPhone at any accepting point of service in place of your card. This way, you don't need to rifle through your wallet to make a payment, you can simply pull up your iPhone. To instantly open up the Apple Pay application, you can tap the hold button on the right side of the device two times.

This will open the application quickly and

allow you to make these payments more easily than ever before.

Child-Friendly Mode:

In order to save your new device from being misused or destroyed by children, the iPhone has a child-friendly option. To activate this mode, you simply need to go to the "Restrictions" section of your device's general settings. From there, you can limit access to specified apps, block in-app purchases, and set an age range for appropriate content as you deem necessary.

Conclusion

The latest iPhone models are some of the most advanced smartphones available on the market today. They had already generated a significant amount of hype and anticipation even before their official launch, and despite their high price, they are on their way to becoming one of the bestselling smartphones of 2019.

Apple will also benefit from launching three variations at different price points in order to help in diversifying its product reach. The new models look beautiful and are all much-valued upgrades to the previous model, the iPhone X, which has been discontinued with the release of the XS, XS Max, and XR.

The new iPhones have larger battery capacities which help to make them even more 'mobile' than previous versions and help them to stand out above other competing devices. Thanks to a fast processor, high RAM, top-of-the-line screen resolution, and many more amazing and impressive features, these models are equally great for professional use, recreation, and even for artistic uses and content creation. The handfuls of novel features in these new models can make their use smoother and more enjoyable, as well as simply streamlining day-to-day life and adding ease to all types of interactions one might encounter. These features can sometimes be confusing, irritating, and sometimes even difficult to understand and use effectively, but hopefully, this book has helped you to gain the tools necessary to do so and gain the most out of your new iPhone and all of its incredibly versatile features.

Description

The iPhone family of products has been known since its initial release of the original iPhone all the way back in 2007. Over the course of the 11 years since the release of the original iPhone and its operating system, the iPhone OS (or iOS) 1.0, there have been a number of advancements and improvements to the technology and designs of these products that have managed to keep the iPhone consistently at the top of the smartphone market since they released.

With all of these improvements to the iPhones over the years, it can be difficult and even seemingly impossible for us to keep track of all of these complicated devices' incredibly broad features and capabilities. The newest additions to apple's very large family of products are the successors to the iPhone X. The iPhone XS, iPhone XS Max, and iPhone XR are packed with useful tools to help you to get the most use out of your phone that you can. The handfuls of novel features in these new devices can make their use smoother and more enjoyable, as well as simply streamlining day-to-day life and adding an astonishing sense of ease to all types of interactions one might find themselves in.

These features can sometimes be confusing, irritating, and even difficult to understand and use effectively.

The Handy Guide For Your iPhone XS, XS Max, and XR is designed to help you to gain all of the tools necessary to understand all of these various features and gain the most out of your new iPhone and all of its incredibly versatile features. This book is meant to illuminate the features of these new devices and their operating system, the iPhone Operating System (or iOS), in great detail. It will include their specifications, pros and cons, tips and tricks to help you use them to their best and fullest capacity, and a clear and differential analysis of the latest products in comparison to their ancestors. By the end, you should possess all of the tools necessary to do so and properly utilize all of the applications and various other features available to you on your new iPhone XS, XS Max, or XR.

Links to Pictures

https://pixabay.com/en/icon-icons-computer-phoneapple-1971130/

https://pixabay.com/en/technology-iphone-x-iphonephone-3068617/

https://pixabay.com/en/iphone-smartphone-appsapple-inc-410311/

https://pixabay.com/en/iphone-x-iphone-x-applemobile-3566142/

https://pixabay.com/en/iphone-x-iphone-x-applemobile-3501731/

https://pixabay.com/en/iphone-ios-apple-6s-pluswhite-1067988/

https://pixabay.com/en/iphone-x-samsung-galaxys8-2957216/

https://pixabay.com/en/smartphone-cellphone-applei-phone-1894723/

https://pixabay.com/en/apple-concert-dark-iphonelights-1836071/

https://pixabay.com/en/conference-workshopiphone-3677032/

https://cdn.pixabay.com/photo/2018/01/11/21/27/desk-3076954_1280.jpg

https://cdn.pixabay.com/photo/2016/12/01/18/17/mobile-phone-1875813_1280.jpg

https://cdn.pixabay.com/photo/2016/11/29/05/08/apple-1867461_1280.jpg

https://cdn.pixabay.com/photo/2017/10/12/22/17/business-2846221_1280.jpg

https://cdn.pixabay.com/photo/2018/03/09/19/36/iphone-x-3212446_1280.jpg

https://cdn.pixabay.com/photo/2018/06/28/11/37/iphone-3503673_1280.jpg

https://cdn.pixabay.com/photo/2017/12/21/20/56/phone-3032551_1280.jpg

https://cdn.pixabay.com/photo/2019/03/06/10/51/iphone-x-4038013_1280.jpg

https://cdn.pixabay.com/photo/2017/12/25/20/14/iphone-3039062_1280.jpg

https://cdn.pixabay.com/photo/2018/06/29/14/03/iphone-3506067_1280.jpg

BOOK 4
THE IPHONE 11
COMPLETE USER
GUIDE
The Complete Handy Guide

Chapter 1: The New iPhone 11 at a Glance

Every tech-savvy individual living within this fast-paced global village called earth would admit that the year 2019 was a great year for the tech industry and that the mobile industry was not left out as it witnessed a lot of growth, improvement and the shipment of new tech solutions and products.

The big giant in the industry – if not the biggest – that is Apple was not left out of the race in technological development, we can as well say that it is leading the race with its release of high-quality gadgets and devices. In 1984 Apple ventured into revolutionizing personal technology when it introduced the Macintosh. Over the years they have come to introduce some of the worlds most sophisticated and reliable software platforms such as the macOS, the iOS, tvOS and the watchOS for their Mac devices, iPhones, the Apple TV and Apple watch respectively.

These technological breakthroughs offer their customers seamless experience across their services such as the Apple store, iCloud and Apple music. From the mac books to the iPhones, Apple has been inconsistency with its ability to match the high aesthetic value in design with optimized functionality. Around mid-2019 the news about the release of the iPhone 11 was all over the internet, and Apple users and fans could not wait to lay their hands on and have a glimpse at the much-anticipated iPhone 11. So, fast forward to the 20th of September 2019, the new iPhone 11 was released in all its glory. Just like the iPhone X and iPhone XR, the new iPhone 11 did not disappoint at all. iPhone 11 users are surely going to enjoy every cent spent on purchasing this great mobile device as the seamless integration of optimized hardware and reliable software technologies would offer their customers unparalleled user experience.

This revolutionary phone is setting a new pace entirely as the next big thing within the iPhone industry, as it is equipped with a lot of not just new, but useful features. It incorporates amazing new capability with that top-notch design the brand is known for, new additions include the wild and ultra-wide cameras to give your videos and pictures that touch of perfections. The biggest and what seems to be the greatest addition as it directly affects performance is the powerful and yet easy to use iOS 13 operating system, this also comes with the A13 Bionic chip which Phil Schiller claims to be the fastest chip ever installed in a smartphone. Well, if you're wondering who Phil Schiller is, that is the senior vice president of worldwide marketing at Apple. With the rate at which people want to get things done as fast as possible, you wouldn't want to end up wielding a good-looking but inadequate phone that takes forever to load certain apps and to accomplish your daily tasks. The A13 Bionic chip would ensure that your everyday task is handled efficiently.

Image Credit: apple.com

This book will provide you with tips and information on what to expect from your new iPhone 11 and how to use most of its major features.

Chapter 2: Buying the New iPhone 11

It was on September 10 when the news of the launch of iPhone 11 took the internet by storm, and just after a few days after the launch, the device was released on the 20th of September. The much-awaited iPhone comes in six beautiful colours and at a reasonable price of 699 US dollars. Almost every important feature that you can think of as necessary for your everyday task has been improved on. This includes an improved battery life to last you throughout the entire day with just a single charge, a water-resistant design, and upgraded chip to help with some of the demanding tasks iPhone users would want to perform. The most talked-about feature – the dual-camera system – this new camera design is intuitive and promises to give users an exceptional video and photo experience both during the day and at night, as the performance of the night mode feature seems to be have been improved on massively.

The iPhone 11 is made available in memory size models of 64GB, 128GB, and 256GB. As usual, it ships in the two major colours for most phones, and that is the black and white colour. You also get to choose from four other beautiful colours to match your personality, i.e the purple colour, the yellow colour, the colour green and lastly the flashy red colour. The 128GB model is priced at 749 US dollars and the 256GB model sells for 849 US dollars. Earlier iPhone customers can acquire the iPhone 11 through the iPhone Upgrade Program, with a monthly payment of about 29 US dollars per month, customers can get the 64GB model, while the 128GB version can be acquired with a monthly payment of about 31 US dollars, if you want to get the 256GB model, then you should be willing to pay about 35 US dollars monthly for it. Apple customers in the United States and within more than 30 other countries could purchase the iPhone 11 from an approved Apple authorized reseller from the 20th of September.

All new iPhone 11 customers who make a direct purchase from Apple would be offered a free personal setup within the Apple store. This would include helping you to erase data from the old device, transferring useful data into your new device, setting up user accounts such as your email and providing you with useful tips on how to make the most out of some new features. If you choose to buy your iPhone 11 from the Apple store using the Apple card, you would get a 3 per cent daily cash, you can also extend your limited warranty using AppleCare+, this would give you a 24 hours a day and 7 days a week access to their technical support team, with priority access.

There are many platforms where you can learn more about the new iPhone 11, but the new Today at Apple session is the major Apple platform where you can leverage on 15 minutes drop-in session to learn quick tips and tricks on how to maximize the capabilities of the iPhone 11 on interesting topics such as photography and video recording/videography using your iPhone.

Chapter 3: Deep Dive Into the iPhone 11 Design

Just after about a year of releasing the iPhone XR, which received a high level of acceptability within the Apple user's community. The big tech giant went ahead to release yet another device that ticks off all the important checklists for a great mobile device. The new iPhone 11 features the Liquid Retina High Definition Display, which is a 6.1-inch LCD display. This comes with a maximum brightness value of 625 nits, a contrast ratio of 1400:1, and a resolution of 1792 by 828 at 326ppi. This makes it a great mobile device for taking quality photos that are sharp and clear enough to reveal as many details as possible when zoomed in closely. The true tone support feature would give your images that extra touch of professionalism when properly used to adjust the white balance to the ambient lighting

Image Credit: apple.com

The iPhone 11 has a glass body design material that comes in six different colours of white, yellow, purple, green and red, with the purple and green colour been new colour additions to the iPhone brands in 2019. It appears the millennials are beginning to have some sort of consideration in the design of Apple products or someone in charge of that decision-making process is beginning to conquer his fear of colours, whatever the case may be I can certainly see that as a step in the right direction for the big tech giant as this is going to rule out one edge some other brands have over them, even though we know that the iPhone brand is uniquely set apart from other mobile phone brands. Although the iPhone 11 does not come with the 3D Touch just like the iPhone XR, it incorporates the Haptic Touch which is also very efficient as well as the iOS 13 platform supports the Haptic Touch even though it lacks that much-needed pressure sensitivity of the 3D touch.

Looking at the iPhone 11 and comparing it with the iPhone XR, you might not spot much difference except for the dual camera in iPhone 11, but when it comes to design criteria, the iPhone 11 is miles way ahead of the iPhone XR. The iPhone 11 comes with glass material that is said to be the toughest glass ever used in making a smartphone, this boosts the overall durability of the iPhone 11 and offers it improved water resistance. According to Apple, the iPhone 11 was tested by professionals under controlled lab conditions and this was done at a maximum depth of 2 meters for about 30 minutes i.e. at a rating of IP68 based on the IEC standard 60529. Although this test confirms the iPhone 11 to be splash, dust and water-resistant, you should also be aware that the splash, water and dust resistance test was performed within timeframes and that continuous exposure of your device to such conditions would surely decrease its ability to resist over time due to the effect of wear. So, don't go out taking a swim with your iPhone, just because it is water-resistant, you should also take note that Apple won't cater for liquid damage as it is not covered under the warranty. Whenever your phone gets submerged in water, make sure you dry it up properly before usage, you can always refer to the instructions on the user guide for cleaning tips, also make no attempt to charge your iPhone when it gets wet.

Let's explore some features of the iPhone 11 camera. The dual-lens camera is the most visible feature that sets the iPhone 11 apart from the iPhone XR. This introduction is a great improvement over the single-lens camera. It offers you the standard wide-angle shot camera settings and then the new ultra-wide-angle camera setting that offers you a field of view of 120-degree. That is indeed an amazing feature that would serve a great deal of purpose for those who would love to use their iPhone 11 in taking sharp and colourful pictures that would be so realistic and show a great level of details when zoomed into. Although the telephoto lens of the iPhone 11 Pro and Pro Max are not available for the iPhone 11, the dual-lens camera – when used properly – can still give you a great output, so be sure to check out the guides on how to get the best out of your iPhone 11 camera.

Unlike the iPhone XR that only supports portrait mode for person shots only, the iPhone 11 has been upgraded to support different portrait mode shots. This means you can set up both the wide and ultra-wide cameras to shot portrait modes for pets, people, your laptops or any other object you might want to capture in memory. The ultra-wide-angle camera's exceptional ability is not limited to taking selfies and images of your cats alone, it is also ideal for taking some nature photos, so don't limit your adventure. Apple claims that the ultra-wide lens can capture up to four times more scene than the conventional single-lens camera, so using it for some landscape photoshoots and architectural shots won't be such a bad idea at all.

The simple principle behind this exceptional ability of the ultra-wide camera is that the camera interface of the iPhone 11 was upgraded with devices that offer you a more immersive experience, so you would be able to see beyond the boundaries of your frame. This is also complemented with the 2x optical zoom and supported with the digital zoom of up to 5x.

Have you always envied the Google Pixel device just because of its Night Sight mode that allows you to take some pretty cool photos at night? Well if you're getting the new iPhone 11, I don't think you should have any reason to desire the night mode camera ability of the Google Pixel devices. Apple has provided its customers with an improved Night Mode feature in the iPhone 11 that built with great capabilities to process out good quality images within a low lighting environment. The ultra-wide range camera lens and the night mode feature will all combine to produce a crisp and clear photo at night.

Within the information technology industry, the next big thing is artificial intelligence and machine learning. Every big tech industry and institutions are exploring ways to improve their products and services by leveraging on the huge advantage artificial intelligence and machine learning has to offer. Therefore, we are beginning to have self-driven cars and more and more jobs becoming automated through artificial intelligence. Apple has found a way to integrate machine learning into the iPhone as the Smart HDR leverages on the machine learning ability to capture natural-looking images and improving features that give images that touch of realism, such as a high level of shadow and highlight detailing. The iOS 13.2 has been developed with a Deep Fusion technology that takes advantage of machine learning technology in pixel by pixel processing of your pictures. This offers users of the iPhone 11 better photographic experience as the textures are optimized and background noise and grains are also minimized. Generally, when compared to the iPhone XR, photos taken by the iPhone 11 are improved with much detail and to a large extent, barring the photographic skill of the user.

A lot of people love making videos using their iPhones, it is almost becoming a trend these days, as a considerable percentage of vloggers rely on their iPhones to create amazing and engaging contents across various platforms. Trust me when a professional makes a video using a good iPhone like the iPhone 11 and iPhone 11 Pro, you would hardly believe it as shot using a mobile device. This gives users the advantage of having to carry their mobile device wherever they go and as well as having a powerful camera device. The 4K video recording is improved with an extended dynamic range of sixty (60), thirty (30) and twenty (20) frames per seconds (fps). You can also make your video recordings using both the single lens and the dual-lens cameras, and even though you begin with one and want to switch to the other, you can easily do that by simply tapping on your screen through the live swapping property. With the QuickTake video feature, you can press down on the camera app shutter button to track your subject while video recording, while the Audio Zoom feature helps to produce more dynamic sound by matching the audio with the video framing. The new iPhone 11 is also supporting the Dolby Atmos sound system and is built with the new spatial audio feature that is specially designed to simulate the surrounding sound to offer the user a more immersive sound experience. All these technologies put together offers you a great sound output that you can hardly get in any other mobile device.

The new improved features in the iPhone 11 are also taking "slofies" to an entirely new level with the front-facing TrueDepth camera setting that supports 120 frames per seconds slow-motion video for the very first time. So, you can enjoy taking slow motions selfies and adding Hollywood styled slow motion touch to your videos. This ability to capture slow motion is due to the upgrade of the iPhone 11 TrueDepth camera with a whopping 12-megapixel camera that increased the efficiency of the Face ID by up to a 30 per cent increase in speed and an ability to capture from more angles. With the true depth camera, you can have more natural and realistic looking images as it supports the next generation smart HDR and can record 4k videos at a frame rate of 60 fps.

The iPhone 11 looks like the iPhone XR in so many ways, but there are some physical changes in design that you can spot when you compare both phones. The iPhone 11 just like the iPhone XR is designed with a 7000 series aluminium frame that is machined to precision. This aluminium material covers the phones glass enclosure. At 6.1 inches, the display dimension for the iPhone 11 is a little above the iPhone Pro's display dimension, which is at 5.8 inches, while the iPhone 11 Pro Max has a higher display dimension of 6.5 inches. More comparison between the iPhone 11 and other devices would be discussed later in the book.

The iPhone 11 is an all display mobile device except for the speaker, ambient light and Face ID camera notch. There are no home buttons on the iPhone 11, and it has an edge to edge display that is complemented by a slim bezel and a notch is installed at the top to operate the TrueDepth camera system. Since the iPhone uses the LCD display in place of the OLED display, the bezels are a little thicker than that of the iPhone 11 Pro and Prom Max models.

Just like many other iPhone designs, Apple has maintained that portability of iPhones in the design of the iPhone 11. The new iPhone 11 weighs around 6.84 ounces which almost the same weight as the iPhone XR. This weight reflects good material design capabilities within the iPhone's hardware engineering department, as they have found a way to integrate the lightweight but very effective hardware devices into the design of the iPhone 11. This makes the phone very handy and ideal for everyone, as you can simply drop it into your pocket and not feel like you are carrying a dumbbell in your pockets. The dimensioning is also very key to its portability as it measures about 150.9 mm in height, 75.7 mm in width and it has a thickness of about 8.3 mm. This dimension is quite identical to that of the iPhone XR, while the thickness is higher than that of the iPhone 11 Pro and iPhone 11 Pro Max by 0.2 mm.

If you're an iPhone XR user and you take a first glance at the iPhone 11, you would certainly notice one major difference when you turn the phone to its back and that is the camera. The new square-shaped dual-lens camera could be said to be the design ace up the sleeve of the Apple company before the release of the iPhone 11. The dual-lens camera is enclosed with a square-shaped bump that gradually flows into the rest of the phone casing. Since the camera elements are thicker than the phone body, the dual lenses protrude above the body of the phone, but this slight bulge also adds to the aesthetic appeal of the iPhone as it blends in smoothly into the rest of the surface. Another major change you would notice when you look closely is with the Apple logo. The Apple logo's position has been changed from the usual top corner which is common to previous designs and has been moved to the centre of the phone. Most reviewers are of the opinion that this change in design is due to the planned implementation of a two-charging system feature that later did not see the light of the day. Had this new two-way design feature been successful, this would mean that the iPhone 11 would have a bilateral wireless charging system that would power other apple devices such as the Apple Air pods and the Apple Watch.

The last design feature we would in this chapter is the durable glass material of the iPhone. This was designed using what Apple calls the dual ion-exchange process, for those of us who do not have any background in chemistry or material design, it simply means that the result is a stronger glass material to protect both the front and the back of the iPhone 11. According to Apple it is the most durable ever used for a smartphone, so this means better durability and an ability to withstand accidental drops and adhesion against some surfaces. But you should also handle it with care as it is still glass though. To secure your iPhone 11 better it is advisable you get a matching case for your phone, the paddings provided by such cases offer a lot of protection to your phone by damping out the effect of bumps and falls. Secondly, you should also get an AppleCare+ just in case you experience accidental damage to your iPhone. We would explain some of the requirements and nitty-gritty for the AppleCare+ in the next chapter.

Chapter 4: Everything You Need to Know About Apple Care and the Apple Care +

There are those of us who are just too clumsy and are most likely to drop things mistakenly even our mobile phones included. Well, you don't have to feel bad or blame yourself cause that is a mistake most people make occasionally. But even though you shouldn't feel bad about it, the is some serious cause for concern when you purchase the iPhone 11 worth over 600 US dollar. That is why Apple introduced the Apple Care phone warranty plans. Am sure those of you who don't really know much about the Apple Care would be asking questions such as, what exactly is this AppleCare+? Is it necessary for all iPhone users and if so, what makes it very important?

Image Credit: Phone Arena

What is Apple Care and AppleCare+?

To begin with Apple Care and AppleCare+ are not the same thing as most iPhone users are fond of interchanging both words, thinking that they mean the same thing. That plus sign that differentiates them means something that adds a huge difference to various coverages. So, let's get down to the bottom of both coverages.

Apple Care is termed the Limited Warranty Coverage by Apple. Apple Care is what everyone gets whenever he or she purchase any Apple product, this is not limited to the iPhone devices, it includes all Apple Watches, Air pod devices, the Apple TV and even the Mac books. You can call it the baseline warranty coverage for purchasing any new Apple products. On the other hand, the AppleCare+ does not come free for all iPhone customers, this is an add-on service that is paid for.

Just like with every other mobile phone brand or product manufacturer, the warranty is a form of fault or damage coverage that is given to the customer. This is a guarantee that the device or product is expected to work fine within a specific timeframe without developing any fault in functionality. If anything goes wrong with the device within that period and it certain that it was no fault of the user, the manufacturer takes up the responsibility of fixing the device and returning it into a functional state at no cost to the customer. So, Apple Care is simply a product warranty, Apple has only found a fancy name to give it. Since Apple is a company that produces both hardware and operating systems that are truly integrated across various products. Only the Apple Care or AppleCare+ can really afford you access to experts who would offer you a one-stop solution to your iPhone issues.

Features and Benefits Surrounding the Apple Care Warranty

Like most manufacturers, the length of coverage is within a set time limit after which the company signs off taking such responsibilities, and for Apple, there is usually a one-year warranty on all their products. This warranty covers any form of damage or breakage that is no fault of their customer or the iPhone user in this case. So, complaints like my power button randomly stopped working, the mouthpiece seems to be faulty or some factory-installed software seems not to work as it should, would all be entertained within that period. But when you drop your phone and the screen shatters, just know it that such damages are not going to be covered even for a single day after purchasing your iPhone, as it would be deemed a user fault damage.

The Apple Care warranty is also transferrable from one user to another. This means that if you buy an Apple device and decide to resell to someone else, the new user would enjoy the remaining warranty period. For example, if you purchase the iPhone 11 and then decide to resell it to another user after five (5) months of usage, the Apple Care coverage would automatically be transferred to the new user to enjoy the remaining seven (7) months of coverage on the device.

The Apple Care warranty is applicable to all Apple devices irrespective of where you purchased them, so far as they are certified distributors of the device. This means that even if you bought your iPhone 11 from

Amazon or from XYZ store, you would get the complete Apple Care coverage and all its benefits as though you purchased your iPhone directly from an Apple store.

Features and Benefits Surrounding the AppleCare+ Warranty

Now that we understand all about the Apple Care warranty coverage and what all Apple customers stand to benefit whenever they make a purchase. So, what happens when you want an extra warranty or coverage for your iPhone, just in case you accidentally bump it against a hard surface, or it drops. You would simply opt-in for the AppleCare+ coverage which is available for those who simply want to extend their warranty coverage timeframe for the one year to let's say two years. This means that whatever fault your iPhone develops within the period of two years that is not as a result of a mistake on your own part, would be taken care of by Apple. If you also want to add extra coverage to your free 1-year warranty, such as the glass screen shattering as a result of your iPhone dropping, you can do that with the AppleCare+ warranty coverage plan.

To enjoy the accidental damage coverage of AppleCare+, you simply pay a fee to upgrade from Apple Care to AppleCare+. This payment is based on the Apple material that you purchased, be it an iPhone, an Apple Watch or a Mac book. This upgrade can come in handy as most accidental damages would cost you more than the payment for the AppleCare+ subscription.

Let me take you through a quick rundown on the cost of AppleCare+ coverage on some Apple devices. The information provided below is the coverage fees for Apple products as discovered through detailed research and survey. The information provided is to guide as to what you should expect the coverage fee to be as they are subject to changes by Apple.

The iPhone 11, iPhone 11 Pro, iPhone XS,

iPhone XS Max and iPhone X coverage fees are set at 199 US dollar. The fee for iPhone XR, iPhone 8 Plus and iPhone 7 Plus is 149 US dollar, while that of the iPhone 8 and iPhone 7 is 129 dollars. For the MacBook and MacBook Air, you can get coverage at 269 dollars, while coverage for the 13-inch and 15-inch MacBook Pro goes for 269 and 379 US dollar respectively. For the Apple Watch series, the coverage fee for series 4 is set at 79 dollars, while that of series 3 is at 49 dollars. The coverage for iMac is 169 dollars and the Mac Mini is 99 dollars. The Apple TV and Home Pod have a coverage fee of 29 and 30 dollars respectively.

Paying for these coverages does not automatically mean that you can always take your phone for repairing no matter the number of times it gets damaged as a result of an accidental drop or scratch. You should go through the terms and conditions as provided by Apple. Most times you are likely to get only up to two numbers of incidents of accidental coverage as a result of your fault, and there are deductibles per device as well. For any iPhone model, the deductible for any form of screen damage is 29 dollars, while other damages outside screen breakage are 99 dollars. For the Mac Book series, the screen damage deductible is 99 dollars, while other forms of damage are 299 dollars. For the iPod Touch, the Home Pod and the Apple Watch, the deductibles for any form of damage is 29 dollars, 39 dollars, and 69 dollars respectively.

Another form of useful coverage that the AppleCare+ provides is the theft or loss coverage. Enrolling in this coverage allows you to replace a lost or stolen iPhone. To get this coverage you would have to pay an extra fee in addition to the AppleCare+ coverage fee for each iPhone device. For the iPhone 7 and iPhone 8, the fee is an extra 800 dollars, while every other later iPhone version i.e. the iPhone X series and iPhone 11 series are all set at an extra 100 dollars.

Just like the regular AppleCare+ coverage has deductibles, there are deductibles for the AppleCare+ theft and loss coverage. The deductibles for the iPhone 6, 6S, 7 and 8 is 199 dollars, while that of the iPhone XR, 8 Plus, 6S Plus and 7 Plus is fixed at 229 dollars. For the iPhone X, the XS, and XS Max, the deductible is 269 dollars, the iPhone 11 Pro and iPhone 11 Pro Max, is also at 299 dollars.

Having to pay for deductibles and AppleCare+ after purchasing an expensive iPhone is not so desirable. But the cushion effects it would have in the advent of any damage or loss of your iPhone would be very substantial. Imagine losing your iPhone 11 and having to spend about 269 dollars for a replacement as against the full cost of a new iPhone 11. You would be saving over 400 dollars in that process. The question of whether you should get an AppleCare+ is entirely up to you and is dependent on how you use your iPhone. If you know you are prone to dropping your phone or bumping it against a hard surface, you should consider getting an AppleCare+ coverage, and if you are forgetful like so many other individuals who are always having to deal with so many activities in a fast-paced environment, you should consider getting an AppleCare+ Theft and Loss coverage as that extra coverage fee could save you a lot when something eventually happens, you can take it as a form of "phone insurance". One other thing you stand to benefit is that peace of mind, where you are assured that you have your iPhone covered. Whatever the case may be, whether you're getting an AppleCare+ or an AppleCare+ with Theft and Loss, you should ensure you handle your device properly and keep it safe always to avoid loss. It is better to be on a safer side by going through all the terms and conditions of the AppleCare+ coverage, so you know what is applicable.

For the Apple Theft and Loss coverage, it is required of you that at the time of theft or misplacement of your iPhone you should have the Find My iPhone feature enabled on your iPhone, although there may be certain exclusions from this. Just as it is important for Find My iPhone to be enabled on your device during the theft or loss process, it is also important to ensure that your iPhone is associated with your Apple ID during that process as well, as the process of getting you a new iPhone includes erasing the information on your missing iPhone, disabling it and transferring ownership to your newly issued device. Ensure you can always remember your Apple ID and password as you would need that to sign in to your Find My iPhone account, so make sure you always keep your account information up to date. You can also add an extra level of security by using the two-factor authentication login for your Apple ID, but it if you are doing this it is also recommended you link your account to another trusted phone number that you can receive the secured six-digit verification code needed to sign in to your account if you lose your iPhone.

How to Buy Coverage for your iPhone 11

You can purchase coverage immediately you buy your iPhone 11, or you can buy it within 60 days of purchasing your phone. To set it up, turn on your device and go to *Settings*, then select the *General* settings tab and open the *About* phone section and choose the AppleCare+ coverage. You can also use the online support platform to chat with a customer support agent who would put you through the entire process. Lastly, you can decide to visit an Apple store closest to you. For the last two options, it is required you have your serial number and proof of purchase as diagnostics and inspection would be carried out on your phone.

How to Contact Apple to Kickstart your AppleCare+ Coverage Benefits

Once you need any form of repair or replacement, there are various ways you can reach out to the customer support team. As an Apple customer with an AppleCare+ coverage plan, you have 24 hours a day and 7 days a week priority access to their customer support experts, and if you stay in any metropolitan area around the world you can be assured of getting the same day service.

You also have the express replacement service, so you would spend minimal time without an iPhone, as a replacement would be shipped to you, so you don't have to wait for the repair. I would explain more about the express replacement service shortly.

You can send your iPhone to Apple by mailing it in using the apple prepaid shipping box, and you can also decide to use the Carry-in repair method by taking your iPhone to the nearest Apple-authorized service provider.

AppleCare+ Express Replacement Service is available for your iPhone 11

This feature is a benefit that is enjoyed by

Apple customers who acquire the AppleCare+ coverage. When you request for the express replacement, Apple sends you a replacement for your iPhone 11 immediately as well as packaging to help you return your damaged phone for proper repairs.

The Cost of Express Replacement Service

When you order for the express replacement service using your AppleCare+ coverage plan, you would only have to pay for the replacement service, as Apple covers the express delivery for you. Just as explained earlier on all rules guiding the AppleCare+ and Apple Care also apply to the express replacement service. So, whenever you're requesting for a repair that is not as a result of an accident and your warranty period has not elapsed and you request for an express replacement service you need not pay any fee.

How to Return Your Original iPhone

Once you request for the express replacement service, a new iPhone would be shipped to you with factory settings and other necessary information. You are to return your original iPhone to Apple within 10 working days of requesting for a replacement in order to avoid paying late fees. Usually, when you make a request for an express replacement service, you would permit a temporary authorization on your credit card. This covers the complete replacement value of your iPhone and becomes invalid or expires if your repair issue is covered under the normal Apple Care warranty and you were able to send back your original product with the specified 10 business days. If you fail to send your damaged iPhone to Apple within 10 business days after you received the replacement or you did send it but Apple never received it, you would be charged the full replacement amount, and this would be deducted from your card. If after your phone arrives late and the fault is covered under warranty, then the replacement value initially deducted would be refunded to your account and only the late fee would be charged.

Replacement Amounts and Late Fees for iPhone 11

Here is the corresponding replacement value and late fee for iPhone 11, iPhone 11 Pro and iPhone 11 Pro Max.

iPhone 11 64 GB, 128 GB and 256 GB all have a replacement value of $ 699, $ 749 and $ 849 respectively, while their late fee is $ 150, $ 175 and $ 225 respectively.

iPhone 11 Pro 64 GB, 128 GB and 256 GB all have a replacement value of $ 999, $ 1,149 and $ 1,349 respectively, while their late fee is $ 225, $ 300 and $ 400 respectively.

iPhone 11 Pro Max 64 GB, 128 GB and 256 GB all have a replacement value of $ 1,099, $ 1,249 and $ 1,449 respectively, while their late fee is $ 250, $ 325 and $ 425 respectively.

Renewing Your AppleCare+ Coverage

Once your AppleCare+ initial yearly coverage expires, you can always renew or subscribe to a more flexible monthly plan. For example, if you subscribed for an initial 24- or 36-months coverage and this time elapses, you can switch to a monthly basis coverage payment. The monthly plan keeps renewing automatically until you cancel the plan. Once your first coverage of 24 or 36 months ends, you can no longer subscribe for a yearly plan except the monthly plan. To check your coverage status, you can log in to mysupport.apple.com using your Apple ID and selecting your device. Another option is for you to open the Apple support app on your iPhone 11. Then you sign in to your account and tap on Check Coverage.

Chapter 5: The Powerful iPhone 11 Processor

At the annual Apple's event when the iPhone is launched, the vice president of the silicon engineering at Apple Sri Santhanam said that the chip for the new iPhone 11, the iPhone 11 Pro and the iPhone 11 Pro Max is the most performant chip ever built for their iPhones. When compared to previous iPhones processors, the new A13 is said to boost performance by at least a 20 per cent increase. This upgrade includes both the main processor and other engines that support the AI and graphics display.

Image Credit: Techtalk.vn

The design of this new iPhone saw a massive increase in the number of transistors used for an iPhone. From the previous 6.9 billion transistors of the previous year, the new iPhone 11, iPhone 11 Pro and Pro Max are composed of a total of 8.6 billion transistors. The function of transistors in a mobile device or any other computer device is very essential as it is the very fundamental component of that determines the processing power of your computer chips. The more of them you have, the more efficiently you can execute your tasks. Your phone apps begin to speed up and experience no lag at all and your graphics display is also improved.

The new iPhone 11 processor is an A13 bionic 7-nanometer chip that also comes with a neural engine that is third generation. The previous version used in the iPhone X series, that is A12 was at a lower performance rate of 20 per cent compared to the new A13 processor. This improvement is not limited to the CPU only as the GPU has improved in its efficiency as well. These improvements in performance are largely due to the new machine learning accelerators, that was introduced to increase the efficiency of the CPU as it can now perform over 1 trillion operations within just a second. This improvement in efficiency has also increased the neural engine speed in processing graphical related functions on the iPhone such as improving the video display, giving users a better gaming experience by preventing gaming lags, and improving the real-time photography experience by giving you clearer snapshots and selfies with as many details as possible.

Since Apple designs its own chips, it can optimize their designs, and this means that they can determine how to integrate their chips together to form a very efficient package, how many silicon valley estates can be mapped out for specific tasks such as improving the graphics and AI, prioritizing user experience design and reducing power consumption. This advantage of running the entire production stack is a key component in the huge success behind the A13 processing power as it allows them to maintain a steady performance advantage over other top-end Android phones processors even most smartphones are part of the ARM processor family.

In the earlier days of manufacturing microprocessor, improving chips was a less lot trickier than it is now, as present chip makers are constantly looking for ways to shrink transistors to smaller sizes while still coming up with a more efficient design. This usually comes at a high cost of manufacturing. To achieve this efficiency, apply for works with the Taiwan Semiconductor Manufacturing Corporation TSMC to build smaller and yet high-performance chips. The Taiwan Semiconductor Manufacturing company employs new techniques in enhancing them, this includes miniaturizing them and the coupling of memory in a tighter way to improve the overall performance.

The great reduction in the size of the iPhone chip started remarkably with the A12 processor, which was used for the iPhone XS, the iPhone XR and the iPhone XS Max. These Apple mobile devices were the first to be built using the Taiwan Semiconductor Manufacturing Corporation's second-generation 7-nanometer manufacturing process. To understand or have an idea on how deep their manufacturing process and chip miniaturization is, let us compare that to the size of a virus which is about 50 nanometer in width. Manufacturing a chip that small is quite remarkable as it requires a lot of technical expertise in manufacturing. According to Sri Santhanam, the A13 processor's second-generation 7-nanometer manufacturing process produced a chip that is much more powerful and very efficient even at the reduced size. The main A13 processor comes with other four smaller processors to handle low-power processing such as background task. This takes the load off your battery, so it lasts longer. Sri Santhanam also noted that the power consumption of all engines was reduced by a whopping figure of 40 per cent. With the improvement in battery life the iPhone 11 lasts for one extra hour when subjected to the same battery load with the iPhone XR. You can enjoy at least 10 hours of watching some of your favourite movies and videos on your iPhone as it allows up to 17 hours of video playback from the device memory and supports at least 10 hours of video streaming. You can enjoy listening to your favourite artist tracks for long hours with audio playback of 65 hours. The iPhone 11 comes with the standard 5W charger and just like the iPhone 11 Pro and iPhone 11 Pro Max, the iPhone 11 enables fast charging, although this would require extra charging equipment.

The iPhone 11 is designed with an Intel modem chip that is of the Gigabit-class LTE. Other features include a 2x2 MIMO and LAA, a Bluetooth 5.0 and Wi-Fi 6 support (802.11 ax) feature. Included also is a dual SIM slot with the eSIM option and the U1 ultra-wideband chip to improve spatial awareness and enable better indoor tracking. From the iOS 13.1 chip design, the iPhone has been improved through machine learning to suggest directions for Airdrops. This simply means that all you would do is to point your phone to any other iPhone user you want to share files with, and Airdrop would do the rest.

In later chapters, we would review more on the changes in design and platform performance between the previous iPhone X series and the iPhone 11 family.

Chapter 6: Setting Up Your New iPhone 11

So, your ordered iPhone just arrived and it's fresh out of the box, and you begin to ask yourself. "what do I have to do next?". Well, I have you covered as am going to breakdown the top first things you should do with your iPhone to get it all set up for you to enjoy.

Step One – Turn on Your Phone

The first thing you should do after getting your new iPhone 11 is to get rid of your previous phone. Yeah, you can just throw it into the thrash – Just kidding anyways – before you go discarding your old phone, just know that there are safety measures you would have to follow to ensure that your information is safe, we would discuss this in a later chapter. Now, back to the first step in setting up your new iPhone. Getting rid of your previous phone means turning it off, cause the aim of setting up the new one is to move your information from your previous version of iPhone to the new one.

Once you're sure you've turned off your old iPhone, the next thing you need to do is to power your new iPhone 11. This is quite straight forward; all you should do is to locate the power button on the right side of the phone. Then press it down until the Apple logo appears, then you let go of the pressure. The phone should boot up in no time with its improved processor. Once the phone comes up, you can take a deep breath and behold it in all its awesomeness.

Step Two – Choose Your Preferred Language and Location

When the phone comes up successfully, you should be greeted by a welcome screen, slide up this screen to start up your configuration. The next thing is to select the English language and your country of residence. Am assuming English is your language of choice as these instructions are in the English language. You can select any preferred language of your choice and proceed with the next step but know that from this point your choice of language affects everything on your phone, including date, time calendar and contacts. After selecting your preferred language, go ahead and choose your country or region.

Step Three – Setting Up Your Accessibility Option

Next step is to set up your accessibility option, simply tap on the blue accessibility button to continue. If you don't find these next steps necessary, you can jump to the next step on launching the QuickStart.

Step Four – Using the Quick Start

Apple has made setting up the Quick Start as easy as possible for iPhone users with iOS

11 platform and above. If you are using an iPhone with an iOS 13 or later platform such as the iPhone 11 with an iOS 13 platform, all you need to do is to bring the two phones together to begin the automatic set up. If you have any iPhone with an earlier iOS, you would have to use the manual set up. To access this tap on the Set Up Manually button.

Step Five – Activating Your Device

To Successfully activate your phone, make sure your SIM card is on your iPhone, as you would need to connect to the Wi-Fi or any other network service. Tap on the available Wi-Fi you want to connect to get started.

Step Six – Setting up FACE ID or Touch ID

The Face ID and Touch ID are the key settings that offer you a good level of security on your iPhone, so it is one of the first things you should not fail to set up whenever you unpack your iPhone 11. The Face ID and Touch ID security would be used whenever you want to unlock your iPhone 11 or make some online store purchases or other forms of transactions. When the Face ID option comes up, simply tap on the continue button to proceed and set up your Face ID or tap Set Up Later in Settings if you intend to do it later. Once you tap on Continue, you would be prompted to enter a passcode, this would ensure your Face ID or Touch ID is not changed without your permission. Enter your six-digit passcode to secure your data and provide you alone with the ability to unlock your iPhone 11. If you would like a custom code or you want a four-digit code tap on the Passcode Options. (You would also get the option of using no passcode at all). But be aware that your iPhone 11 is more secure with your passcode, it is better to use a supposedly simple passcode than using no passcode at all. I have provided more information on the apple Face ID and Touch ID in the following chapters.

Step Seven – Transferring Your Information and Restoring Data from Old Devices

From the Apps and Data section, you can retrieve your data from your iCloud and iTunes account backup into your new iPhone 11. You would have the option to restore from your iCloud Backup, your Mac or PC, to transfer directly from iPhone, to Move Data from Android. If there are no backups for you to transfer into your iPhone 11, select the Set Up as New device option to proceed. You can read up more informative tips and procedures on data transfer and migration on your iPhone 11 in subsequent chapters.

Step Eight – Login with Your Apple ID

On the Apple ID page, you would have the option to sign in with your Apple ID in order to use iCloud, iTunes and other Apps from the App store. Enter your Apple ID and continue or tap on the Forgot Password button to retrieve your Apple ID and password. Don't have an Apple ID? You can use Don't Have an Apple ID tab to create your own Apple ID. For users with their Apple ID's signed into other devices, you might be prompted to enter a verification code form your older iPhone. If you use more than a single Apple ID across your Apple Accounts, you can use the Use Different Apple IDs for iTunes and iClouds to login with the proper Apple ID into the separate accounts.

Step Nine – Allowing Automatic Updates

When you continue with allowing the automatic updates, you would get the latest features and security updates. You would be notified automatically of any improvements or iOS upgrades. IF you do not want to share your information with app developers by turning on automatic updates, you can choose the Install Updates Manually, so you can decide when to check your iPhone for new apps and iOS upgrades. Turning on the automatic updates does not mean you won't have any restrictions on the installation of the updates. Before any update is installed you would be sent a notification and you can choose to allow updates or discontinue the automatic updates from the Settings.

Step Ten – Time to Put Siri to Work

Siri is the Apple AI that would serve as your device assistant, all you would do is to say Hi Siri or press down on the side button to get Siri to work, as Siri is willing to help you get things done if you ask. Simply press the Continue button and follow the instructions to complete the setup, you might need to say a few words or phrases, so you and Siri can get to know each other, as Siri works better when it knows its owners' voice.

Step Eleven – Configure the Screen Time

With the Screen Time configuration, you

can get a weekly report to give you insights on how much screen time you or your kids spend on your iPhone. You can also manage your apps by setting time limits and parental controls on children's apps. You can read up more information about Screen Time in the next chapter. Once you're done setting up the Screen Time, you can tap on the Continue button and toggle on the True Tone. You can adjust the size of your home screen icons using the Display Zoom. The iPhone 11 enables you to use gestures to navigate through your device.

Once you're done setting up your screen time, you can go on to start using your device. The Apple user guide is always there for you to refer to.

Chapter 7: Detailed Guidelines and Steps on How to Configure Your New iPhone 11

In the previous chapter, I gave a brief description on how to get started with your iPhone 11, these included a brief step by step break down on how to set your passcode, perform data transfer, create a Face ID or Touch ID and lots more. In this chapter, I would provide you with detailed steps and information about some of the initially discussed setting and how to go about making more advanced setups that would improve your experience with your new iPhone 11 and get you started without much stress.

Setting Up Your Accessibility Option

With iOS 13, you can easily set up your

accessibility option. You can easily zoom in for clarity using your iPhone 11 or any other iPhone running iOS 13. To zoom in, you just need to enable zoom in by tapping the screen twice with your three fingers. Another option is to turn on the Voiceover feature, that would help you with the instructions if you have low vision. To set up the voiceover feature, press the side button three times and hold on for the voice prompt that the voiceover has been enabled. For models earlier than the iPhone X, you can use the home button in place of the slide button.

Other options that help you to navigate through the entire process includes:

The Display and Text Size which gives you the flexibility to adjust text size, contrast and transparency.

Spoke Content helps to read out all the text on your screen, you can also select the range of texts you want the speaking feature to catch.

Motion settings feature acts more like the mouse sensitivity settings on a PC, you use this to reduce excessive user interface motion, you can also use it to turn off message effects and video previews.

Touch Settings enables the Assistive Touch and other Touch functionalities.

Switch Control is useful for highlighting screen elements that can be activated through an adaptive accessory.

The Keyboard configuration gives you a customized typing experience when you connect an external keyboard to your device.

Now, you can go back to setting up your accessibility options after tapping on the blue accessibility option.

How to Use the Quick Start

What the QuickStart basically does is to use information gathered from your old iOS device to set up your new iPhone. You can then drop your content and data from iCloud backup into your new mobile device. Before you begin the process, please avoid the mistake most people make by wanting to continue using their old device while the QuickStart process is on, as they think it is only the new iPhone that is affected. Quick-Start would be on both devices whenever you trigger on the transfer process, so ensure you pick a time when you won't be needing both mobile devices.

Here are the steps to follow for you to set up your Quick Start:

Make sure your Bluetooth features are turned on and that both devices are running iOS 11 and later, then turn on the new device and place them side by side or very close to each other. The Quick start-up would load up on your old iPhone and then prompt you to use your Apple ID in setting up your new iPhone. Sign in with the correct Apple ID and tap the continue button.

Once you sign in, some animation is going

to appear on your new iPhone, then place your older iPhone over the new one and try to centre the animation on the screen to the viewfinder. You should get a message prompt that says Finish on your new iPhone. If you get an error message preventing you from using your old iPhone's camera, press the Authenticate Manually button and follow the next steps that appear.

If stage 2 is successful you would be asked to enter your old iPhone's passcode unto your new iPhone. Once you're done with this proceed to step 4 below.

Next, step is to set up the Face ID on your iPhone 11. This step is straight forward, simply following the step by step instructions would achieve the desired result.

You would be prompted to enter your Apple ID into the new iPhone, you would also have to enter the passcodes of your various Apple devices if you have more than one.

Once you've successfully entered the right Apple ID into your new iPhone, you would have the option to restore information that includes your apps, data and settings from your last iCloud backup. You would also get the second option to update your older iPhone back before restoring the data. To enable your new iPhone to pull data from the iCloud storage make sure your Wi-Fi device is turned on. Then you can select a backup and filter down how you want to transfer your settings, that is either by Apple Pay, location and privacy.

Wait for the transfer to finish and your new iPhone 11 would become updated with your previous settings and information.

Using the iPhone Migration for Direct Data Transfer

Am sure you were excited when you heard about being able to use the QuickStart to set up your new iPhone 11, so far as your previous device runs on iOS 11 as also. Well, if you want to transfer data between two phones with iOS 12.4 and above, there is more reason for you to get excited as you can transfer data from your old phone to the new phone wirelessly or by connecting them together. If the wireless network you are using for the transfer is quite slow or congested, you still have the option of choosing the wired method.

To use the wired method for your migration, you need the following; the first is the Lightning to USB 3 Camera Adapter, while the second is the Lighting to USB Cable. The Lightning to USB 3 Camera goes into your old iPhone, while the Lighting to USB Cable goes into your new iPhone 11, and the other end goes into the adapter. Then plug the Lighting port of the Lightning to USB 3 Camera to a power source with at least 12 W supply or above.

Here is the step by step process on how to use the iPhone Migration:

Put on your iPhone 11 and place it close to

your old iPhone running iOS 12.4 or later. If you would like to transfer the data using the wired connection means, connect the wires as explained earlier on. As usual, you would get the Quick Start screen that would ask you if you would like to use your old iPhone's Apple ID to set up your new iPhone 11. Enter the right Apple ID you intend to use and press the Continue button to proceed. If after entering your Apple ID and you don't get to see the continue option on your old iPhone, check to see that the Bluetooth is on, if not turn it on.

If the previous step is successful, an animation should appear after a while on your iPhone 11. You are to place your old iPhone over your new iPhone 11 and try to place the animation in the centre of the viewfinder. Wait for a moment and you would get a successful message saying Finish on your iPhone 11. You might have issues using your old iPhone camera, tapping Authenticate manually and following the proceeding steps would most definitely solve the problem.

Next, you should be prompted to enter a passcode on your new iPhone 11, you should enter the passcode for your old iPhone here.

Once you've entered the passcode successfully, you can now follow the instructions to set up your Face ID or your Touch ID on the new iPhone 11.

Now is the time to transfer your relevant data from your old iPhone to your new iPhone 11. So, choose the settings you want to transfer from your previous iPhone to the new iPhone 11 such as Siri, Apple Pay and privacy settings.

While the transfer is going on you would be prompted if you would like to transfer data from any other device into your new iPhone 11 such as an Apple Watch. So, use the opportunity to transfer all settings and data that you want to be updated on your iPhone 11.

Throughout the whole transfer process, you

should keep both devices close together, and do not forget to perform the data migration when you won't be needing either of the phones. To make sure that both phones have adequate power to complete migration, it is advisable you connect them to a power supply as the transfer process takes a considerable amount of time to finish.

Allow the transfer to finish up and your migration is complete.

Chapter 8: Finishing Up Your iPhone 11 Settings

There are a few other settings you might need to do to complete your iPhone setup. After successfully migrating your data you might have to re-enter your passcodes to your Mail App, Contacts and Calendar App.

To begin, go to Settings, then open Password & Accounts.

Next, select each of the accounts and then enter your correct password when prompted.

Check Mail, Contacts and Calendar App

I would advise you to check if your Mail, Contacts and Calendar are up to date.

To begin, launch the Mail App and allow

your emails to download to your new iPhone 11. Enter your email password when prompted to do so and proceed to set up your email.

For the Contacts App, once you open it check to see that all your contacts from the previous iPhone were successfully transferred.

Next, open your Calendar App and check if all your events were successfully transferred, if not you can use the iCloud to update your calendar events.

Enabling Notifications

Asides the Mail, Contacts and Calendar apps, you might need to open some other apps to enable their notifications. Once you open any app and you prompted to, tap Allow Notification. If you open anyone and cannot allow it's notification, you would have to do that from the settings. So, go to Settings and navigate to Notifications, then open notification for the app.

Bluetooth Accessories Pairing

Another setup you would want to do is to pair your Bluetooth accessories such as your speakers, Air Pods and headset. To do this, go to your Settings to open the Bluetooth and turn it on.

Now turn on any of your accessories that you want to pair with your iPhone 11 Bluetooth and put that accessory on Discovery Mode, then wait for the accessory name to show up on your iPhone 11.

Tap on the accessory name to pair it with your iPhone 11 and enter your passcode when prompted to do so.

Adding Your Credit/Debit Card to Apple Pay

For you to be able to use Apple Pay on your new device, you would have to add your debit card, prepaid card and credit card to your Wallet.

To do this go to your Settings and navigate

to Wallet & Apple Pay.

You would see the plus (+), tap on it to add a new card.

Follow the instructions on how to enter your card details and their security codes. You may also need to download your bank or card issuer's mobile app before you can successfully add your card to your wallet.

Once you have successfully entered the correct details of your cards, you bank service provider or card issuer would run a check on the information provided to verify your card. You might be required to provide more information or might be required to input a confirmation code from your bank. Once you have the information, go back to your Wallet and tap on your card to enter the details.

Once the verification is done, tap next to complete the process. To add other cards, repeat the same process, you can add up to 12 different cards on your iPhone 11.

Adding your card to Apple Pay makes payment easier with your iPhone, as your card can be used for payments on the Safari browser and you can send money to family and friends using your Apple Pay.

Managing Subscriptions

A subscription in this term is what you pay to access content from a website or an app over an agreed period. For example, you can subscribe on Apple Music to get access to some music of your choice, you can subscribe to Apple News+ for daily news updates, and you can subscribe for Apple TV channels, Apple Arcade and so on. This subscription is not limited to Apple alone as you can subscribe to other third-party contents such as Spotify, Hulu, HBO Now and so on.

For most of these apps and other services, you would have to pay a subscription fee by subscribing to a monthly or yearly plan for you to have access to their content. Most times once you link your cards to these subscriptions, they renew automatically until you cancel them yourself. So now that you have linked your card to Apple Pay, you might want to manage those subscriptions.

Using the iCloud to Keep your iPhone 11 Calendar up to Date

The Calendar update is another advantage the iCloud offers iPhone users, with the iCloud your calendar is always handy. Changes made to your calendar does not only update on your iPhone, but it also updates on every device connected to that account. When you properly manage your events using your Calendar, you won't have to miss any appointments or meetings as you would be right where you need to be and when you need to be there. Here is how to perform default Calendar setting on your iPhone 11. To that open your Settings and navigate to your Calendar, then choose from the list of options on what you want to make your Default Calendar. Note that whenever you create any new event, your iCloud will add this newly created event to your default calendar automatically. So, you should consider setting a Calendar you use the most as the default. You can as well change your default calendar whenever you wish to, all you would do is to follow the previous steps on how to set up your default calendar. Once you are done setting up your default calendar from your mobile phone, the next thing you should do is to make the same settings on your iCloud account. To do this log on to iCloud.com and go to Calendar and locate the Settings icon, next open the Preferences and choose your preferred Default Calendar from there and tap on Save. With this, you can always make changes to your default Calendar settings using both your iPhone 11 and your iCloud account from any other device.

Managing Your Calendar Through Adding, Changing and Deleting an Event

Managing your calendar or schedule of events is quite easy and straightforward. Whatever changes you make using your iPhone would reflect on other devices immediately. To add an event, open your Calendar under settings and select the proposed date of the event. Tap on the plus sign and enter relevant information about the appointment or event. Editing a created event is just as simple as creating the event, to do this go to your Calendar and select the event you would like to edit. Update the event with the right information and save it. Having a lot of events can be a little bit distracting, as receiving constant notification from some events you don't seem interested in can be annoying, most especially when they occur frequently like getting weekly reminders. To get rid of these unwanted events, open your Calendar and select the unwanted event and tap Delete

Event. The Calendar only permits you to delete events you created yourself. To remove events created by someone else such as meetings, you would have to Decline that event from the Invitation sent to you, afterwards you can then go ahead to remove that event from your calendar. Another tricky kind of notifications or events to delete are subscriptions. Using the Calendar subscription is a very handy way of staying up to date on current trends in sports, social media and so on. But like I stated initially when this becomes too much, you might lose out on the very important event notifications. To delete a subscribed Calendar event from a social media website such as Facebook, firstly you would have to unsubscribe from that event. To unsubscribe from any Event on your iPhone 11, open your Calendar under Settings. Tap on the Calendars button and open the button with the information symbol. The information symbol is an "i" symbol with a circle round it□. You can then press the Delete Calendar to unsubscribe from the unneeded event. Once you have successfully unsubscribed from the event, you can then proceed to delete it from your Calendar by following the earlier steps on how to delete events from your iPhone 11 calendar.

Sharing Your Calendar with Family and Friends

With the Family Sharing feature, you can create a family group, more like a social media chat group. But this functions basically to track your family members schedule, your family members here are those who have been added to a group. Every family member can set appointments and would also be able to see everyone's schedule. Any changes made by a family member would update automatically on every member of the group's device.

How to Change Your Time Zone

If you have a 3:00 p.m. event on your calendar and you then travel from San

Francisco to New York, the event is going to alert you by 6:00 p.m. due to the three hours' time zone difference between San Francisco and the New York. Your iPhone checks for your current time zone and automatically updates all your initially set events to align with that time zone. If you don't want this automatic update, you can override this in your iPhone 11 Calendar Settings.

To do this, launch your Settings and navigate to the Calendar. From here locate and open the Time Zone Override, then use the slider to turn on the Time Zone Override.

Once you are done, you can then press the Time Zone button to get a list of the available Time Zones. Choose your preferred Time Zone and that's all, your Calendar event would now retain its initial Time Zone and notifications would sound at the initially set time.

Managing Contacts on Your New iPhone 11

In this section, you are going to learn how to manage and delete contacts on your new iPhone 11.

- Setting Up Your Contact Accounts

The first thing to do is to link up your email accounts contacts to the Contacts App. You can set up your contacts' accounts such as your business directory.

First, open your Settings and tap on Password & Accounts. Then choose Add Account, select your email account and turn on Contacts. To add other contacts accounts like CardDAV and LDAP, tap on Other. Enter your details and password when prompted to do so, then tap Next to finish.

- Turning Accounts Contacts on or Off

If you have already set up an account and you want to remove the contacts, follow these steps to turn off the contacts.

Locate the Settings and choose Password & Accounts. Then choose the account with the contacts you intend to add or get rid of. For adding contacts, simple toggle the Contacts button On. If you want to remove contacts, simple toggle the Contacts button Off and the press Delete Account to erase.

- Setting Up Default Account for Adding New Contacts

Since you can set up multiple accounts on your Contacts App, you would enjoy the ease of use if you choose a default account where you want your contacts to be saved. Follow these steps to choose a default account for your new contacts. Go to your Settings, then open the Contacts and tap on the Default Account. This would bring up all your contacts account for you to choose your default contacts account.

- Change How You Filter Through Your Contacts Display

Here is another setting that can greatly

improve the ease of use of your iPhone 11. This has to do with changing how you sort out your contacts either alphabetically using the last name or first name. To do this open your Settings and choose Contacts. There are three options for you to choose from and here are there functions.

Option one is the Sort Order which arranges your contacts based on the alphabetical ordering of the first name or last name.

Option two is the Display Order that displays the first name of your contacts before or after their last names.

Option three is the Short Name which enables you to sort out how you want your contacts names to display in apps like Mail, and Messages.

- Deleting Contacts

There are moments when you just realize you have gathered up a lot of contacts that were once relevant but have become a bit useless to you overtime and you want to delete them to make room for more. Before deleting your contacts bear it in mind that they would be permanently deleted from your device, and that anyone deleted from your email account would be deleted from all devices signed to that email. So, if you're sure you want to proceed, follow these steps. Go to your Settings and open the contact to be deleted, then tap edit and scroll downwards to the end of the page and tap on Delete Contact, if you are sure that's the contact you want to delete you can proceed to tap Delete Contact again to confirm it's deletion.

Effectively Using the Screen Time on Your iPhone 11

The Screen Time setting offers you the ability to have real-time access to your activities on your mobile device as you can view the weekly report on how much time you have spent on your iPhone 11. It offers you the leverage of setting time limits on mobile device usage, these settings come in handy when you feel you are beginning to slide downwards the slope of mobile usage addiction, most especially in using fun apps such as games. Screen Time is not for phone owners only as it gives parents the ability to set parental control for their kids as well.

Using the Screen Time to know how much time you and your kids spend while using your iPhone to navigate through fun apps and websites, would go a long way in helping you make more informed decisions on your mobile phone usage principles.

To navigate to the Screen Time, go to Settings and open the Screen Time tab. Turn it on and tap Continue to proceed. You would then have the option of selecting My Device or This is My Child's Device. There are two ways to create restrictions on your child's device, the first is to do that on their iPhone, while the second option is to do that through your own iPhone 11 using the Family Sharing Setting. The Family Sharing feature also enables you to view reports and tweak settings on your child's mobile device right from your own iPhone. To ensure that you alone have access to changing the Screen Time settings, you can create a passcode to authenticate any form of changes such as extending screen time. It is advisable you choose a passcode different from the one you use in unlocking your phone.

To create a passcode for the screen time, open your Setting and go to the Screen Time feature where you should see your wards name. Click on the child you want to adjust screen time setting for and tap on the Change Screen Time Passcode to create a passcode. You would be required to authenticate the change using either your Face ID, Apple passcode or your Touch ID. IF you want to take off the Screen Time passcode simply tap o the Turn Off Screen Time Passcode.

To use the Family Sharing, when you open your Settings, navigate to the Screen Time and open Set up Screen Time for Family. Follow the instructions provided on how to set up your Screen Time Family and add a child to your family. You can always add family members or children through the Family Sharing feature. From your own device, you can then get reports anytime you want and adjust the settings as required. Since you are in control you can share music, games, movies and other apps that are safe for your kids to navigate through.

The Screen Time provides you with a detailed report on your device usage, including apps opened and websites visited, so to view this detailed report just go to the Setting and open up the Screen Time, then Tap the Sell All Activity under the graphical representation. From here you can get a quick glance on which apps you have used the most and decide if it is necessary to set some sort of limit on that app. If you want to get information on all your devices that are signed in with your Apple ID, for example, if you want to view the report on your iPad using your iPhone 11, toggle on the Share Across Devices button.

There are four major settings you can adjust, and they are the Downtime, the App Limits, the Content & Privacy Restrictions, and Always Allowed.

Downtime

The Downtime is setting a period when you put all phone functions to a halt, except for phone calls and apps which you excluded from the downtime. The downtime only has control over the apps that you have enabled Screen Time for. You would be given a five minutes notice before the downtime begins, and your screen time apps go to sleep.

App Limits

The App Limits helps you choose what app you want to limit its usage. One very good scenario is limiting gaming apps and social networking apps that limit your productivity. This could be done when you feel a sense of addiction for yourself or your kids to a gaming app, or you feel you need to be more productive at work, so you want to limit your chatting, twitting and texting. By midnight every day, your App limit refreshes, and you can choose to extend or end the limits anytime you want to.

Content & Privacy Restrictions

The Content and Privacy Restriction section are where you would want to make the most adjustments if you would like to protect your kids from been exposed to inappropriate content. With this, you have control over the kind of content that appears on your iPhone and you can block downloads and prevent purchases. You don't want to be that mum who would wake up one day to see that her daughter just ordered a truckload of her favourite toys, using her card. So, the earlier you set those restrictions the better.

Always Allowed

There are apps you feel that are always useful and you don't want them turned off for a moment. The Always Allowed feature helps you keep such apps functional so you can always have access to them even when the downtime triggers on. These Apps would remain turned on even when you turn on the All Apps & Categories app limit on. By default, the Phone Call, Phone Messages, FaceTime and Maps apps are always allowed, you can still choose to remove them.

Parental Control Tips for Your Child's iPhone

As explained earlier on in the Content & Privacy Restrictions, you can limit app usage and protect your child from getting exposed to explicit content and making purchases with your phone. In this section, I would provide steps on how to set content and privacy restrictions, how to prevent iTunes and App Store purchases, how to block explicit contents and prevent downloads.

How to Set Up Content and Privacy Restrictions on Your iPhone 11

To begin open your Settings and go to Screen Time. Then tap on Continue, you would have to choose between My Device, and This is My Child's.

If you're making changes from your ward's device, choose the My Child's option and follow the instructions until you are prompted to enter and confirm the Parent Passcode. If you want to restrict through your iPhone, you can use the Family Sharing feature to restrict a family member. To prevent someone from changing your settings create a Screen Time Passcode if you've not. Simply tap on the Use Screen Time Passcode to create a new one.

Once you're done with the previous step, go ahead to open Content & Privacy Restrictions. Enter your password when prompted to do so and then turn on the Content and Privacy button. Now that you've turned on the Content and Privacy, let's go through how you can manage some of the settings earlier discussed.

Preventing Purchases From the iTunes & App Store Purchases

This setting would help you prevent your child from making in-app purchases, installing unwanted apps or deleting any apps.

To begin, open your Settings as usual and go to Screen Time. The tap on the Content & Privacy Restrictions button and enter your passcode if asked to do so.

Next, open the iTunes & App Store Purchases. You should get three Store Purchases & Downloads options. If you want to prevent your kids from installing apps, set the Installing Apps to Don't Allow, and if you want to prevent your child from making purchases set the In-app purchases to Don't Allow, and the same goes for the Deleting Apps settings. For the Required Password setting, you can choose to require a password for additional purchases by checking the Always Require button.

Preventing Explicit Contents

You can prevent your kids from exposure to explicit content, music and TV shows by filtering out contents with specific ratings.

To begin go to your Setting and open the Screen Time, navigate to the Content & Privacy Restriction and tap on the Content Restrictions. Then choose the type of content you would like to restrict.

Here is a breakdown of some of the contents you can restrict:

Ratings For: With this, you can select the approved rating for a country or region and apply those contents ratings automatically.

Music, Podcasts & News: You can use this to filter out music, podcasts, and music videos containing inappropriate wordings and contents for kids.

Apps: This would help you block apps that have a specific rating, such as violent games that are not appropriate for kids within a certain age range.

Music Profiles & Posts: This is where you can prevent your kids from seeing what their friends are listening to.

Other content restrictions include the TV shows, Books and Movies where you can stop them from reading books and watching movies and TV shows with certain ratings.

Adjusting Web Content Settings

The iOS 13 in iPhone 11 has been optimized to automatically filter through your website content and prevent access to adult content in your Safari browser and phone apps. You can also manage the settings to filter through it manually by adding a specific website you always want to allow through.

Open your phone Settings, go to the Screen Time and open the Content & Privacy Restrictions.

Enter your Screen Time Passcode when prompted to do so and then tap on Content

Restrictions.

Navigate to the Web Content and open it up. You would have three options which are to give Unrestricted Access, to Limit Adult Websites and Allowed Websites Only.

If you want your iOS to filter out adult contents automatically, check the Limit Adult Websites.

To enter in specific websites that you want to prevent, check the Allowed Websites Only and use the Add Website button under the Never Allow section to prevent such websites.

Preventing Siri Web Search

Here is the final adjustment you might need to make pertaining to managing your web content.

Open your Settings and go to Screen Time. Then open the Content & Privacy Restrictions and tap on the Content Restrictions. Navigate down to Siri and adjust the following settings.

The first is the Web Search Content, which you should use to stop Siri from searching the web for answers when you ask a question.

The second one is the Explicit Language that you can turn off to prevent Siri from displaying any explicit language.

Restricting Gaming

With the improvement in processor power and GPU engines, iPhone 11 users are now open to so many options when it comes to gaming. Playing games is good as it can help you relax, but when you begin to spend the time that should have been channelled into more productive ventures on gaming alone, then you need to start considering some forms of restrictions. As adults it is easier for us to say no to excessive gaming, but we know that is not the same for kids as they lack that same amount of will power, so setting restrictions in gaming would go a long way in helping them stay focused.

To begin, locate the Screen Time feature under your Settings. Then go to the Content & Privacy Restrictions and open the Content Restriction page. Navigate down to the Game Center to start making changes.

You can prevent any form of multiplayer games on the iPhone under the Multiplayer Games section.

Under Adding Friends, you can stop your child from adding friends to the Game Center

You can also prevent game screen and sound recording as well using the Screen Recording feature in the Game Center.

Chapter 9: Things to Do Before You Give Out Your Old iPhone

Before you get all caught up in the euphoria of getting a new iPhone 11 and exploring the numerous features the new phone has, there are a few steps, guidelines you need to follow to sell properly, trade-in or give away your old iPhone. This is to ensure the safety of your information. In this section, I would explain how you should go about removing your personal information from your old iPhone in a safe manner. Don't make the mistake of having to manually delete your information such as your documents, contacts, calendars, photos, and videos. Doing this manually while you are signed in to your iCloud account using your Apple ID would delete these files and data from the iCloud server, and you won't be able to access it on any device connected to that iCloud account. To erase your data securely, follow these steps.

Step 1

First thing you should do id to unpair your devices from your old iPhone, such as your Apple Watch. You would find detailed steps on how to do that below.

Step 2

Once you have unpaired your devices, you should make sure you have backed up your device so that you would have all your updated information on iCloud. You can find details on how to back up your device below.

Step 3

After successfully backing up your device, you can then sign out of iCloud and the iTunes & App Store.

If your device is running an iOS 10.2 or earlier, go to your iPhone Settings, open iCloud and tap the Sign Out button. Press the Sign Out button again and tap Delete from my iPhone, you would be required to enter your Apple ID password for confirmation. Once you are done with the iCloud, go to your Settings, open iTunes & App Store and tap on Apple ID, then tap on Sign Out.

For iPhone devices running iOS 10.3 or later, you have a much simpler procedure. All you would do is to open your phone Settings and tap on Your Name. Navigate downwards and tap on the Sign Out button. Input your Apple ID password and tap on Turn Off, and you're done, you have successfully signed out of iCloud and iTunes & App Store.

Step 4

After signing out of iCloud and iTunes, you can now erase your data securely. Go to your Settings and open General settings. Press Reset and tap on Erase All Content and Settings. You might be required to enter your Apple ID password if you have Find my iPhone turned on. You should be prompted to enter your device passcode, once you do this you can then tap on Erase.

Step 5

You may contact your carrier to help transfer services to the new owner.

So, what if you have already given out your phone without performing the steps listed above. Well, there are things you can try out to keep your data safe.

The first option is for you to contact the new owner of the phone and ask the person to follow the steps listed above to help erase the content.

Another method is for you to sign in to iCloud or Find My App using another device, you can use your new iPhone 11 for this. For this to work, your old iPhone should be connected to your iCloud and Find My App. Sign in to iCloud or Find My App on your new device, select the old device and tap on Erase. Once the process is done, choose Remove from Account to unlink the old phone from having access to your iCloud information.

If you cannot get across to the new owner of the phone and you don't have it on your iCloud and Find My App, you may choose to reset your Apple ID password. Changing your Apple ID password won't erase any of your personal information on the old device, it would only prevent the new owner of the old device from deleting contents from your iCloud.

If you are using the Erase All Content and Settings from the old iPhone as explained in the five steps of erasing your data, all iCloud services would be turned off and the information on your device would be erased completely. So, asides your photo, music, apps, and contacts, it would also erase all your debit and credit card details that were added to your Apple Pay account and this data wipes off on your old device would not affect your iCloud content.

Now, if you are using Apple Pay on the old device and you were unable to do this erasure, you would have to unlink your credit and debit cards from that device. To begin, launch iCloud.com, choose settings, you should see a list of your devices connected to your iCloud. Choose the device, next to Apple Pay and tap on Remove to unlike the device from your card.

How to Unpair Your Apple Watch from Your Old iPhone

Note that unpairing Apple watch would restore it back to factory settings.

To begin, place your old iPhone close to your Apple Watch. Then navigate to the Apple Watch app on your iPhone and tap on the My Watch tab.

Select the Watch you want to unpair by tapping on it, next press the □ to bring up the Watch information.

Press the Unpair Apple Watch button to

take you to the next step.

If you're using the Apple Watch Series 4 or Series 3 with both GPS and Cellular connectivity, you should choose to keep your plan since you might want to keep your plan.

Confirm your selection and enter your Apple ID password, and with that, you have successfully unpaired your Apple Watch from your iPhone.

Erasing Apple Watch

If you would like to erase your Apple Watch data, open Settings from your Apple Watch, go to General and tap on Reset.

Next, choose Erase All Content and Settings and tap Erase All to confirm your selection.

Backing Up Your iPhone

Backing up your device save a copy of your information so you can retrieve it when you want to switch to a new device due to replacement or loss of the previous device. Here are steps on how to back up your information using iCloud.

The first thing to do is to connect to a good internet service such as a Wi-Fi network.

Open your Settings and tap on Your Name under your profile picture. Navigate to the iCloud button and open it.

Once iCloud is open, toggle the iCloud Backup button on and tap the Back Up Now button.

Make sure you remain connected to a good network until the entire back up process is completed.

To confirm if the back up is complete, you can check the progress under the settings. Open your phone, Settings, and tap on Your Name. Then navigate to the iCloud page and tap on the iCloud Back up. On this page, you would find the date and time of your latest back up under the Back Up Now button.

Chapter 10: Using Face ID on Your iPhone 11

The face ID is a layer of security that helps you gain access to your iPhone and can be used to sign-in securely to apps and authenticate purchases from Apple Store.

Before you begin setting up your Face ID, you should ensure that your TrueDepth camera is not been covered by any particle and most especially ensure that nothing is covering your face. So, get rid of anything you normally won't be using on your faces such as face caps and glasses. But if they are things you would normally be wearing such as prescription glasses and contact lenses. It is okay to have them on as the Face ID has been designed to work with them.

Follow these steps to set up your Face ID:

Step 1

Open your iPhone 11 Settings and navigate to the Face ID & Passcode.

Enter your passcode and then tap on Set Up Face ID.

Step 2

Hold your iPhone at an arm's length, about 10 to 20 inches distance from your face should do. You should be holding your phone in portrait mode and not landscape. (Just in case this part is confusing to you, portrait position means your phone is the longest top to bottom, while landscape means your phone is longest left to right).

After positioning your phone and your face correctly, tap the Get Started button.

Step 3

Try to adjust your face to fit within the circular frame and then begin to move your head slowly in a circular motion path to complete the green circle round the frame.

If you are having any challenges with moving your head, tap the Accessibility option for help.

Step 4

When you complete the motion, you should get a message saying First Face ID Scan Complete.

Tap the Continue button so you can proceed to the next stage.

Step 5

You would be required to repeat the Face ID scan for the second time, so move your head to complete the circle path. Once completed you should get a message saying Second Face ID Scan Complete.

Step 6

Once you have completed the steps above, you would get a successful message saying

Face ID is now set up. You can now tap Done to exit.

Now that your Face ID is set up, you can go to your Face ID & Passcode under your phone Settings and choose what features you want to be authenticated with your Face ID such as signing into apps and making purchases.

How to Unlock Your iPhone 11 Using your Face

Here are steps on how to unlock your iPhone using your Face ID.

Step 1

Wake your iPhone by tapping on it or using the Raise to Wake. The Raise to Wake is a feature that automatically wakes the Lock Screen of your phone when you raise it up. In case your Lock Screen does not come up when you raise your iPhone 11 to look at it. Go to Settings, open the Display & Brightness configuration and turn on Raise to Wake.

Step 2

Hold your iPhone 11 in portrait mode and glance at it. The Lock icon on your screen should animate from been locked to open.

Step 3

You can now swipe upwards from the bottom of your screen to unlock it.

If you no longer want to use the Face ID screen to unlock, you can turn it off. Simply go to your Settings and navigate to Face ID & Passcode. Tap on the iPhone Unlocks to turn it off or on.

Using the Face ID to make online Purchases

The Face ID can serve as a means of authentication in making purchases from the App Store, and the iTunes store.

To make in-app purchases, follow the steps below.

Step 1

When you are done with picking your items from the app or website on Safari. Check out and tap on the Buy with Apple Pay button. If the option is not available, choose Apple Pay as your method of payment and confirm the payment information before proceeding.

Step 2

If you want to use a card that is different from the default one, tap on the forward arrow ">" next to your card, if not skip to Step 3.

Step 3

Now double press your iPhone 11 side button and glance at your iPhone screen (the side button is the button at the right side of your iPhone if you are holding your phone as you would normally do to operate it). Your Face ID would be scanned, and you would get a successful message saying Done with a checkmark.

For purchases through the App Store, the iTunes Store and Book Store:

Step 1

For you to use the Face ID authentication on your iTunes and App Store, you need to ensure that iTunes and App Store is turned on as one of the features requiring Face ID authentication.

Step 2

When you are in your App Store, iTunes Store or Book Store and you find what you want to purchase, tap on the item to go to the payment page.

Step 3

When you are prompted to pay for the item, double press the iPhone side button.

Step 4

Glance at your iPhone screen and wait for the Face ID authentication to complete, you should get a message saying Done with a checkmark.

Signing in to Apps Using Face ID

Face ID can also be used as a security means to have secured access to certain apps. For example, you can set up Face ID for authenticating usage of apps such as your banking app and other phone apps that hold vital information. It can also be used for auto-filling username and passwords for websites on the Safari browser.

To set this up, follow these instructions:

Step 1

Open the app you want to use Face ID authentication with and tap on the sign-in button.

If prompted to use your Username and Password, select Allow the App to use Username and Password.

Step 2

Next, glance at your iPhone screen to sign

in.

To check which Apps have been allowed to use Face ID, go to your Settings and navigate to Face ID & Passcode, open Other Apps to control which apps you want to use Face ID for.

To use username and password autofill with your Face ID on websites in Safari, go to your Settings, navigate to the Face ID & Passcode and turn on the Password AutoFill.

Now, to use this feature, load your Safari browser and visit the website you want to sign in to.

Tap on the sign in field to prompt you to enter your username and password, tap on it and glance at your phone screen to autofill your username and password.

Chapter 11: Using Touch ID on Your iPhone 11

The Touch ID is another secure means of getting access to your device. Most people would feel this is more convenient and less dramatic since it uses the fingerprint, as against the Face ID that involves you glancing at your iPhone to gain access. Make sure you have created your passcode before you proceed to set up the Touch ID.

Use the following steps to set up Touch ID for your iPhone:

Step 1

Wipe the home button clean using a smooth piece of paper and clean up your finger, making sure there is no dirt or particle sticking on it.

Step 2

Go to your phone Settings and navigate to the Touch ID & Passcode. Type your passcode when prompted to do so.

Step 3

Open the Add a Fingerprint button and press down lightly on your iPhone home screen using your thumb preferably.

Step 4

Hold down your finger until you're asked to lift it up to your finger or when you feel the phone vibrate.

Step 5

Lift and place your finger slowly, changing the positioning of your finger slightly by tilting it to the right, left and so on. So, the phone can capture a wider area of your finger.

Step 6

The last step involves adjusting your grip.

To do this hold your iPhone as you would normally do when you want to unlock your phone. Then press your home button with the outer areas of your fingertip, rather than the centre of your finger that was first scanned.

Unlocking Your iPhone and Making Purchases Using Touch ID

Now that you have set up your Touch ID, it is time to use it in unlocking your phone. To do this, press the home button with the finger you used in registering for the Touch ID.

The Touch ID can be used in place of the Apple ID for authenticating purchases from the iTunes Store, App Store and Apple Books.

To make purchases with your Touch ID, follow these steps:

Step 1

Check to see if the iTunes & App Store is

turned on by going to Settings and opening the Touch ID & Passcode. If you have challenges turning it on, go to Settings, open iTunes & App Store and sign in with your Apple ID.

Step 2

After turning on the iTunes & App Store feature, you can then proceed to whichever store you want to make purchases from, that is the iTunes Store, Apple Store or Apple Books.

Step 3

Choose whatever it is you want to buy by taping on it and you should see the Touch ID authentication request pop up.

Step 4

To confirm the purchase, touch the home button lightly and that would capture your fingerprint.

With the Touch ID, making payment becomes easy as you can even make Apple

Pay purchases from website stores on your Safari and Apps on your iPhone 11.

How to Manage Your Touch ID Settings

Managing your Touch ID settings from your iPhone 11 is quite straightforward, to this go to your iPhone Settings and open the Touch ID & Passcode feature.

From here you can see a list of features that would be requiring your Touch ID authentication, such as the iPhone Unlock, the iTunes & App Store, Apple Pay and Password AutoFill. You can toggle the switch off to disable Touch ID requirement for that feature.

You would also get to see a list of the number of fingerprints you have, as you can have up to a five (5) fingerprints. You can rename a fingerprint by tapping on it to edit its name. To add another fingerprint, click on the Add a Fingerprint button and follow the instruction. But note that the more fingerprints you have, the longer your Touch ID fingerprint authentications would begin to take. If you want to delete a fingerprint, all you would do is to Swipe it to the bin to confirm the delete.

If you want to be sure of the fingerprint you're deleting, or you simply want to rename the fingerprints accordingly to the respective fingers you used to create them. To identify a fingerprint from the list all you would do is to touch your home screen button lightly as usual and you would notice that the corresponding fingerprint would be highlighted briefly.

With the fast-paced technology growth, security is very paramount when you're handling devices that hold your data and carry vital information, so you should make conscious effort to safeguard yourself and your data, that is why I've taken out time to explain how to secure your iPhone 11 within this last few chapters. With that, I believe you know all you need to in order to have exclusive access to your new iPhone 11. In the next chapter, we would be discussing some tips and tricks you can implement to have a better experience with your iPhone 11.

Chapter 12: Tips, Tricks and Updates to Help You Enjoy Your New iPhone 11

Here we are going to look at some of the new features that come with the iPhone 11 iOS 13, and how you can utilize them to get the best out of your new iPhone 11.

Adding a Virtual Home Button

Any previous iPhone user would admit that prior to the release of the new iOS 13, it was almost impossible to imagine using an iPhone without the home button. The expulsion of the home button from the iPhone 11, can startle iPhone users as most of us cannot imagine our lives without it. It is like Apple has literarily taken our home away from us, cause we are used to just pressing the home button when we seem to have come to the end of our adventures and don't have the time to start closing every page or app we open. Now that we no longer have a home button, how do we go home? Well, the answer to this is the use of gestures, and you would enjoy your new iPhone 11 better if you know how to use these gestures as there are so many gestures for different actions. In the next chapter, we would run you through some of the gestures that you should know in order to get the best of experience out of your iPhone 11. But for now, let us focus on how to add our virtual home button.

To do this open your Settings and scroll down to Accessibility. When you open the Accessibility scroll down to the PHYSICAL AND MOTOR tab where you would see the feature called Touch. Tap on it and when it opens, tap on the Assistive Touch button, it should be set to Off by default. Toggle on the button to enable the Assistive Touch, and with that, you should see a digital home button appear right at the bottom of your screen.

With this, you can perform all the functions of the usual home buttons in previous versions of the Apple iOS. You can click on it wherever you are on your phone and it will take you back to your Home Screen. You can access the Control Panel from your virtual home button, and you can even enable Siri and access your notifications from there.

One other special functionality the virtual home button offers over the usual home button is that you can move it around to somewhere more comfortable. To do this simply press down on the virtual home button and drag it to wherever you want it to be, then release your finger to drop it right there.

The New Dark Mode

These days we spend a whole lot of time on our mobile devices. We are either texting, chatting on social media channels, replying emails, playing games and so on. A lot of applications or platform providers are beginning to leverage on our need to have easy accessibility to their apps and services. Therefore, they are building mobile versions of their applications to keep us engaged. All these increases the time we spend staring at our mobile phones and there are times when you just want to give your eyes a break. The new dark mode is the perfect feature to help you relieve your eyes from excessive brightness of the screen.

There are some ways you can turn on the Dark Mode for your iPhone 11. The first one is to go to your phone Settings and open the Display & Brightness section. Under the appearance setting, you would see the light and dark mode with sample images on how your phone would display when you apply either of the effects. Tap on the dark mode to turn it on and watch your iPhone turn from the usual light screen background to a dark background right there within the Settings page.

Another way you can set the dark mode for

your iPhone 11 is through the Control Center. To bring this up, swipe downwards from the top right corner of your iPhone 11. Tap on the dark and light mode icon to switch between dark and light mode for your iPhone.

One other way to turn on dark mode is to ask Siri. To do this, you need to get Siri to listen to you by pressing down on the side button, as usual, you can then say, 'Turn on Dark Mode'. If you are having challenges using this feature, maybe you should go through the instruction on how to Setup Siri. If this is successful you would get a reply from Siri saying "Ok, I turned on Dark Mode", and of course your iPhone should now be in dark mode. When you want to revert to light mode, you can also repeat the same process by pressing your side button and saying turn off dark mode.

What makes the dark and light mode so attractive is how it affects the display of wallpaper. The four new wallpapers that come with the new iOS 13 integrates seamlessly with the light and dark mode like they were specifically designed to bring the best out of the dark/light mode feature. Asides the four new wallpapers, the dark mode also affects other wallpapers as well and you can dim their brightness when the dark mode is turned on.

Another thing that makes the dark mode so cool is how it affects your Apps and their display. It gives them such a powerful and yet comfortable feel. For example, your calendar and notes interface totally change like it was upgraded with new interface design. Some third-party software like twitter has also updated their applications to support the dark mode.

For the best effect try using the dark mode at night or whenever you're in a dark or dimly lit room. You would feel a lot more relief on your eyes.

The 3D Map Feature

This is probably the greatest addition to the

list as there are some cool things you can now do with maps on your iPhone 11. To enjoy the new 3D map, open the Maps app on your desktop and tap on any part of the city you want to view. Now tap on the Map Settings button, which is the topmost icon on the top right corner of the map app. From the Map Setting page, open the Satellite tab. Now tap on the 3D icon which is the last element on the top right corner of the screen. From the 3D map view, you can pan around using two fingers, you can zoom in and rotate to look around. The 3D view gives you a very realistic view, that I can say is quite laudable compared to the google maps street view. With this, you would get a better understanding of terrain you're currently in or about to visit.

The 3D view is not the only update that makes the updated map so amazing. Another great feature of the map is the Look Around feature. This gives you a virtual reality sort of walk around through the area you're currently viewing.

To activate this view, place a pin on the area you want to view. The Marked Location page should pop up above the map. Tap on the Look Around button and you would be given an immersive experience of the location you picked. Another way to open the Look Around feature is to tap on the binoculars icon whenever you see it on your map. The Look Around feature gives you a 360 view of your location. To move to a landmark, such as a restaurant, you can just tap on that point and the map would zoom in to the point. You can also get more information about that restaurant, such as their menus and business details. As at the time of writing this book the functioning of the Look Around feature is currently limited to some states around the US, but Google is working to make it available throughout the US and other countries of the world.

Changing Contact Information in Message

With the changes in the iOS 13, you can

change your iPhone 11 contact information to determine how other iPhone users see your details whenever you are chatting with them.

To make these adjustments, open your Settings and scroll down to the Messages button and open it.

Tap on the Share Name and Photo feature to start making changes. From here you can change your photo and name.

To change your picture, tap on the photo avatar and you would have the option of choosing from a list of Animoji's and taking or uploading your own picture.

Going back to where you have the name and photo options, you should toggle on the Name and Photo Sharing option to allow your Messaging app to share your contact details. You have two options for sharing your information. You can decide to automatically share your information to your contacts only by checking the Contacts only tab or set it to always as by checking the Always Ask.

Ability to Use Some iPhone Features on Other Apple Devices

The iPhone 11 gives you the ability to perform some of its functions on other compatible Apple devices, such as receiving a phone call on your Mac. This feature is great for performing relevant tasks that would normally require you to use your phone, but your iPhone is not handy. Imagine leaving your iPhone in the bedroom and you're somewhere else like in your sitting room working with your laptop, and your phone suddenly rings. Instead of abandoning your position and breaking your workflow by walking down to the bedroom, you can easily pick up your call using your MacBook.

To leverage on this feature, open your Setting and tap on the Phone button. Open the Calls on Other Devices page.

Toggle on the Allow Call on Other Devices button and then choose from the options you have by toggling them on.

To receive messages on other devices as well, go to your Settings and open Messages. Tap on the Text Message Forwarding button to display the devices you can toggle on to receive or send text messages from.

Enhanced Privacy Settings

Just like we all know, Apple is a company that takes data privacy seriously and are always trying to stay atop when it comes to designing systems with high-end security measures.

With the new iOS 13 and iPhone 11, they have taken the data privacy of their customers to a whole new level, with this iPhone users can now force Apps to request their permission in order to access their location. To enable this new feature, go to your Settings and open the Privacy. Tap on the Location Services to see a list of apps using your location. To make an App request for permission rather anytime it wants to use your location, enable the Ask Next Time feature. This extra option is an addition to the two options of Never and While Using the App, which either stops the app from accessing your location when setting to Never or always accessing your location when setting to While Using the App.

Most iPhone users don't know this but there are some apps that are constantly using your Location feature to track you without you knowing it. One other way this is done is through the Bluetooth, where you have some apps using your location information when you allow them access to your Bluetooth. So, when you want to share a photo you can turn off the Location information before sending the picture.

In previous chapters, I explained how you should erase all your data before transferring your old iPhone to another user. If you are a security-sensitive individual and would like to keep your information private. You might want to consider turning on the Erase Data feature. How this works is that when you turn this feature on and there are up to 10 failed attempts to unlock your iPhone 11, all your iPhone data will erase.

To use this feature, open your Settings, Tap on Face ID & Passcode and enter your Passcode when prompted to do so. Scroll downwards to the bottom of the list, you would see the Erase Data feature, toggle the button on to enable it.

I would advise you to make sure you've backed up your data on iCloud before doing this. You can go through the steps on how to back up your data in previous chapters.

The last thing we would be talking about in this section is the ability for you to prevent unknown callers from distracting you. This feature is called the Silence Unknown Callers and it can be very useful when you want to keep your privacy. The world is a global village and even though some websites and applications promise you data privacy whenever you use their application, not all keep to that promise. So, maybe you've filled a form online and have given out your phone number and you begin to receive unsolicited phone calls from telemarketers, scammers, stalkers, spam callers and even wannabe boyfriends. Go to your Settings and tap on the Phone icon, and under the CALL SILENCING AND BLOCKING CONTACTS, you can toggle on the Silence Unknown Callers to save yourself from unnecessary disturbance.

New Document Scanner

If you play around with files and documents a lot, then you are surely going to love this new iPhone 11 scanning feature. You can access this scanner through your Files app on your desktop. Click on the Files app and tap on the Browse button at the bottom right corner of the screen. On the Browse page, you would see three dots at the top right corner of your screen, tap on it to open the options available. Select the Scan Documents button and place any document you want to scan in front of your camera behind your phone. Your iPhone would then try to detect the document you're trying to scan. When you feel the coloured highlight has covered the area you want to be scanned as closely as possible, tap on the round button to capture your image. Now you can move the anchor points around to fit your image properly in the scan area, and once you're satisfied click on Keep Scan to scan the document. To make some edits, tap on the scanned image, from here you can add the black and white filter to make the image look more like it was really scanned using a scanning machine.

Saving Battery Life

The new iPhone 11 already comes with upgraded battery life, but here is a setting you can adjust to improve your battery life, and it is called the Optimized Battery Charging. One thing that reduces the longevity of batteries is excessive charging and this is because some people would plug in their charger and then leave it to charge throughout the night. When you do this, your iPhone would charge up to 100 per cent and your mobile phone would keep receiving power supply. What the Optimized Battery Charging does is that it learns your charging routine. So, when you plug in your iPhone, it charges up to 80 per cent and then waits till about the time you would be needing your iPhone before it charges the remaining 20 per cent.

Exploring the New Animoji and The Updated Memoji

With the update on iOS 13, the iPhone 11 comes with three new Animoji characters, the mouse, the octopus and the cow. These Animojis tracks the movement of your face and then tries to emulate those expressions. The Memoji has been updated with extra facial features such as additional hairstyles, eyebrows, piercings and earrings. You would also gain access to a lot more Animoji and Memoji stickers. Stickers are a good means of making your chat more fun and engaging, asides that they go a long way in adding more meaning to your messages. Texting does not offer that facial expression you would get when communicating face to face with someone. Dragging a sticker to your message would help translate your mood to the recipient. One other cool thing about the updated Animoji and Memoji is that you can access them even outside your messaging app such as your Notes, all you would do is to open your Memoji tab to access them.

The New Quick Path Typing

Here is another amazing feature that the new iOS 13 is offering iPhone 11 users. With this feature, you don't need to download any third-party apps in order to swipe through your keyboard while typing. If you don't know about this swipe typing feature or you've not used it before, it is straightforward and comes in handy whenever you don't feel tapping on your phone keyboard. To use this feature, simply think of a word you want to type and place your finger on the first letter of that word. Now, slide your finger across the screen in a path that would cut across every letter in that word. You can start with short words to get comfortable with it before moving on to more complex statements. The good thing about this is that there is no setting for this, so it is not like you would have to turn off the keyboard tapping to use keyboard swiping, you can use both interchangeably.

Another extra typing tip I would like to offer you, just in case you don't know how to use it yet, is the easy text selection. If you are typing and you want to copy or cut out one word, simply double tap on that word to highlight it for copying. If it is a whole sentence you want to select, triple tap on any word within that sentence. To select an entire paragraph, I believe you should know the flow now, all you need to do is quadruple tap.

Upgraded Safari Download Manager

If you are familiar with the Safari browser for any of the previous iPhones running on any iOS less than iOS 13, you would know that the Safari Download feature is anything but user-friendly. Whenever you click on the download button for the iOS 13, you don't get any sort of confirmation to begin downloads. But for the iOS 13 on the iPhone 11, you would get pop-up information about the file you want to download and requires you to press the download button once more in order to approve of the download. A download manager has also been added to the Safari browser. To access this tap on the download icon at the top right corner of your phone screen when you are in the downloads page. From here you can also open the downloads folder by tapping on the magnifying glass icon.

You can also change the downloads folder

by going to Settings, opening the Safari button and tapping on the downloads. By default, it should be set to saving on iCloud, but you can pick a folder in your local drive to save your downloads.

Using the App Action

Another additional feature to make life easier for iPhone 11 users. This is a very simple feature that lets you get a preview of quick actions you can use your apps for. To use this feature you just have to press down on the app of your choice to get a list of things that app can do for you, then you can select one action and once the app loads, it would take you right into that section of your app. Let's take, for example, the Instagram app. When you hold down on the icon, you would get a list of Instagram functions and this is the Camera, New Post, View Activity and Direct. Rather than opening Instagram and starting from the usual home page. You can jump right into the Camera function.

Purging Multiple Tabs

There are people who just love to keep things simple by opening one tab at a time and would close it immediately they are done, and there are the special ones who are always multitasking. They can open as much as 20 tabs on their Safari browser, it could be a list of items they want to shop online, articles they want to read and so on. What happens is that over time, these pages begin to accumulate, and you would probably have no need to return to most of those pages even if you intended to do so in the first place. Before you realize this you might be having up to 10 or 20 pages that you would have to hit the X button in order to close them up. With this feature, you can program your iPhone 11 to purge out these webpages within a specific time interval.

To use this feature got to your Settings and scroll down to Safari. Navigate down to the TABS section and you would see the Close Tabs. By default, it should be set to

Manually. Go in and change it from Manually to either the After One Day, After One Week, or After One Month option depending on whichever one you feel comfortable with.

Ability to Edit Videos and Photos Better

With the iOS 12 on previous versions of the iPhone, you don't get much editing options for your videos and photos. For the video editing, you can only trim the videos to the desired start and end time. But with the iPhone 11's new iOS 13, we almost have an endless list of video editing opportunities for you to try your hands on. You can trim by adjusting the play backslider when you are in the editing mode. You can add filters and effects such as noise reduction, highlights, shadows, contrasts, intensity, tint and vignette. You can make other adjustments such as modifying the videos aspect ratio and changing its orientation.

Another additional feature is the ability to embed your video edits data to your video whenever you want to share it with your friends. This metadata would enable your friends to see all your original videos and all the edits you have made, whenever you share your video with them. This makes it easier to collaborate with your friends when you all want to jointly edit a video using your iPhone 11. To enjoy this feature go to your Send options and toggle on the All Photos Data.

Something for the Mobile Game Lovers

The introduction of the Apple Arcade for the iOS 13 has offered mobile game lovers a reason not to look elsewhere to satisfy their gaming fantasies. There are a lot of games that you can play, and they come with great qualities and are quite affordable at $5 per month.

Another interesting update is the

PlayStation and Xbox controllers support for the Arcade on the iOS 13 platform. With this you get that flexibility and comfort desktop games would offer you, while you're playing on your iPhone 11.

Saving Up Your Data

There are times when you would have limited data and when you don't manage that you might end up running out of data. There are times when you might have to leave your comfort zone where you have unlimited data supply to someplace where you would be on a metered data usage. For example, you might go on vacation and you won't have access to unlimited data usage. To manage your data, you might need to check some apps silently consuming your data in the background. The iOS 13 comes with a new feature that helps you with this, by activating a metered or low data usage mode, this helps to conserve your data greatly.

To access this feature, go to your phone Settings and tap on Cellular. Here you should see the cellular data option. Open it and toggle on the Low Data Mode option.

Fast Emergency Dialing

No one expects or hopes to be in an emergency where he would need urgent and timely help. As we all know, no matter how safety conscious we try to be there are some situations we cannot control, and that is why you need to put measures in place to salvage such unprecedented events. In any emergency case, every second matter and timely action is required. So, in as much as we don't hope to be in that condition, we also need to put measures in place just in case the unexpected happens.

By default, the emergency and power off feature are triggered on when you press down on the side button and any of the volumes button simultaneously. But you would have to hold it much longer for it to now activate the emergency SOS and dial emergency service.

There is another way that makes this faster as it would only dedicate that process into triggering emergency and not both emergency and power off.

To access this feature, go to your Settings and open the Emergency SOS page. Toggle the Call with Side Button on to activate this command. With this, all you would do is to press the side button five (5) times and it would trigger on the Emergency dial. Turning on this feature, still won't affect the other option of pressing down the side button together with any of the volume buttons as you can use either of the two. But I highly recommend you turn on this button as it is not only more specific to the Emergency SOS, but it is also faster to turn on, all you need to do is to press 5 times.

Once you've toggled on the Call with Side Button, it is time for you to set up your emergency contacts. This step is also as important as turning on the emergency button.

You can set up your Emergency SOS contacts in your Medical ID using the Health app.

To begin to go to the Emergency SOS and locate the Setup Emergency Contacts in Health tab, tap on the button to open and follow the instructions.

How this works usually is that you would add some emergency contacts to your list of emergency contacts, this could be the family doctor, your spouse, your mum or your dad, and even friends you believe could provide adequate help. Once you trigger on the emergency dial by pressing the side button five times, messages are sent across to your list of Emergency SOS numbers, and these messages also carry your location so help can be provided immediately.

Remember, it is better to stay safe than to be sorry at the end of the day. So, make sure you toggle on the button and ask your family members and friends to do the same as well.

Using the Hidden Track Pad

Just like the Quick Path, this is another amazing feature that iOS 13 users are really going to like, most especially if you are going to be doing a lot of typing using your new iPhone 11. To understand how important this feature is, imagine how frustrating it is when you are typing then you realize you need to make corrections, then you start trying to place the cursor right on the letter you want to delete but then you keep missing the positioning by a letter. With this trackpad, you can easily slide your cursor around till you get to where you want to make corrections.

To use this feature all you would do is to press down on your Space Bar whenever you are texting, and you should see your keypad area greyed out. Start moving your finger around to move the trackpad to where you want it to be.

Taking Full Page Screenshot with Your iPhone 11

If you want to screenshot a webpage, we all know how simple and straight forward this is. All you would do is to press on the side button simultaneously with the up-volume button and your screenshot would be taken, very easy, right? But how about when almost everything on the webpage is relevant and you want to capture it all. For previous versions of iOS, you would have to take one screenshot, save it, and then scroll down to take another and keep repeating the process depending on how bulky the webpage content is.

But with the new iOS 13 on iPhone 11, there is a new feature called the Full Page that can take screenshots of the entire webpage. Here is how to use it.

Press down the side button together with the upper volume button as you would normally do to take a screenshot. Now when your iPhone has taken the screenshot, tap on the screenshot image to take it to the editing mode. From here you would see a couple of editing features like annotating your image, highlighting and drawing on it, but those are not what we are looking for. What we need is at the top right corner of the page and that is the Full Page button.

Tap on it and your iPhone would capture screenshots of the entire webpage in sequence just as it is on the website. You can now go-ahead to do whatever editing you want and when you're done, tap on the Done button at the top left corner of the screen to save it on your drive.

Using the Upgraded Reminders App

Looking at the old reminder app of the iOS iPhone versions and comparing it with the newly designed reminders app of iOS 13, you would acknowledge that there was a total overhaul of the reminder app, as the previous design just looked bland. The UI was redesigned to fit more into a modern-day app interface. But the reminders app revamp was not only about better design, but it was also about better functionality. When it comes to staying organized the new reminder app offers you the best possibilities. You can create your own list when you open your Reminder App by tapping on the Add List at the bottom right corner. You can easily add some customization by adding your own colours, avatar and name.

In any of the lists, you can add your reminders by tapping on the New Reminder button at the left corner of the List you chose. You can use the quick toolbar to add some parameters to your activity. Clicking on the clock button icon can enable you to add when the Reminder should go off. You can also click the □ icon to have more options. Take out some time to explore the various options you have there.

To help you stay more organized, you can

create subtasks under a parent reminder. Here is an example of how best to use this feature. Let's say it is a weekend and you have a lot of things you want to do. You want to rush the grocery store, your daughter needs to go to her dance class, you need to take her to the dentist after that, your son wants to go for his football practice, while you need to drop by at work briefly to finish up with some specific tasks.

If I was to organize this using the subtask feature, I would create three-parent reminders, and name them something like. Take Care of Kids, Go Grocery Shopping and Office Priorities.

Now I would create the tasks Pick Up Daughter from Dance Class, Take Daughter to Dentist, Pick Up Son from Football Practice. Then I would make them all Subtasks of Taking Care of Kids.

For Go Grocery Shopping, I would have Eggs, Milk, Veggies, Meat, Butter and so on. While the Office Priorities would have tasks,

I must complete ensuring that the short time I spend at work is worthwhile, I believe you get the entire picture right now. With this method, you can minimize your subtasks and just have those three-parent reminders, and whenever you want to you can maximize to view them.

To make a reminder a subtask of another reminder, simply hold and drag the subtask into the parent reminder. When a parent reminder has been created, you can hold and slide any reminder below it to the right, to indent it into a subtask.

To help you stay even more organized, asides grouping Reminders within a List, you can also group Lists into a Folder. To do this simply drag a List into another List to create a new group.

Chapter 13: Doing Things Faster on Your iPhone 11 Using Gestures

As I explained earlier on, in this chapter I would be explaining how you would achieve some functionalities by using some gestures. In the previous chapter I showed you how you can bring up virtual home button, so here I would be explaining to you how to use gestures to go home, switch between apps, invoke Siri, your Control Panel and so on. The gestures for the iOS 13 have been greatly improved, so whether you're a new iPhone user or a veteran user, you might still need some help understanding some of the new gestures.

Image Credit: Mothership.sg

Going back to Your Home Screen

To back to your home screen wherever you are on your iPhone 11. From the gesture area at the bottom edge of your screen, swipe your finger up your phone display. If you are not a new iPhone user, you should find this gesture to be quite like how you would normally bring up the Control Center. Now that we know how to return to the home screen from any point on our iPhone, we can explore other functionalities without fear of not being able to find our way home.

Switching Between Apps on Your iPhone 11

On earlier versions on the iPhone, you would have to bring up the fast app switcher for you to swipe from one app to the other on your iPhone. With the new iPhone 11 and the iPhone XS, all you would do is to swipe correctly, and you would swiftly move between apps. Most times this should work smoothly, but some older apps might have some glitches so try to run an update all apps to their latest versions. To switch apps, place your finger on the gesture area at the bottom of your iPhone screen and swipe left to right or from right to left.

Swiping from left to right takes you back to previously opened apps, while the right to left swipe takes you to more recently opened apps. This means that once you stop, the last app you opened would be your most recent app and you can only swipe backwards.

Using the Fast App Switcher for Multitasking

If the basic swiping is not so efficient for you to move between apps, then the fast app switcher would provide you with more flexibility and help you stay organized. It also makes it easier to close apps you no longer use. If you're an old iPhone user who is not used to the iOS 13, you might think all you have to do is double-tap the home button or use the 3D touch swipe to bring up the fast app switcher, but these methods are not going to work as there is a gesture to bring up your multitasking interface.

To use the gesture, touch the gesture area at the bottom of your iPhone 11 screen with your finger, then swipe up gently and pause. You don't have to swipe completely to the top of your screen, just a short way up and it should work. You also don't have to swipe fast like you want to flip, this would take you to the home button. Try it a few more times and it will become second nature, it's quite simple. Slide up gently, pause for a moment and your fast app switcher would pop up.

Once you are in the fast app switcher you can easily purge any apps you no longer want open. To do this, simply swipe up on any app you want to close, and it'll be gone. You can also close multiple apps, all you would do is to place a finger on each app and then swipe them all up to close.

Entering Reachability Mode

This is one important feature that some mobile phone users are not taking advantage of. So, whether you are new to the iPhone or a veteran iPhone user like some of us, this is one feature you should be able to make use of at appropriate moments. If you're still wondering what reachability mode is all about, it simply brings your iPhone closer to your fingers, so they can reach it easily. Most times when you want to be very efficient with your phone, you would need to operate them with both fingers, but there are times when you are just tired or probably in bed and you simply want to operate your iPhone with only one hand. If you feel you are never too tired to operate your phone and so won't be needing the reachability mode, why don't you consider the time you spend leaving your toothbrush hanging in your mouth while brushing your teeth and trying to perform some tasks on your iPhone with both hands.

The reachability feature would come in handy at such moments, as you can keep going up and down with your toothbrush on one hand and your finger, on the other hand, can go all over the place on your minimized iPhone 11 display.

To use this gesture, you need to set it up first. To begin open your Settings and tap on General, then open the Accessibility and navigate to Reachability. Toggle the button on to activate reachability. Once you are done setting it up, place your finger on the gesture area at the bottom of your screen and swipe downwards to open reachability.

Staying in Control with the Control

Panel

For users who are not new to the iPhone, you would find the multitasking gesture to be similar with how you would usually open the control panel in older iPhone versions. With the iOS 13, things have changed a little, so to open your Control Panel, your finger should be placed on the top right corner of your iPhone display and swipe down.

Opening Notifications

The gesture for opening your Notifications is like that of the Control Panel, only that instead of swiping from the top right corner of your iPhone display, you would have to swipe from the top left corner. If you're wondering how far is right or left when swiping from the top, you can use your iPhone notch as the demarcation.

Chapter 14: Getting the Best out of the Improved iPhone 11 Camera

The most notable feature the iPhone 11 comes with is it's upgraded camera. According to Apple, the iPhone 11 features a next-generation Smart HDR that recognizes people and improves their appearance by producing natural-looking skin tones and adding the necessary highlights and shadows.

Night mode off   Night mode on

Image Credit: Flickr.com

Another feature of the iPhone 11 camera that I would be running you through on how to use it is the Night Mode. The iPhone 11 Night Mode is designed to give you better lit up photo in low light. This feature is possible due to the larger sensor of the wide-angle camera that has 100 per cent Focus Pixels. When you take pictures in an area with poor lighting, the Night Mode comes on automatically, so you wouldn't need to use your flashlight.

The ability to take Portrait Mode is another great ability of the iPhone 11. The portrait mode photo focuses on the main subject and blurs out the background, more like the bokeh effect you would get using the DSLR camera. Comparing the portrait mode of the iPhone XR with that of the iPhone 11, you would notice that there has been a great improvement, the iPhone XR portrait mode could only recognize people and apply the bokeh effect, but with the iPhone 11 you can focus on almost any other object and blur our it's environment, it could be your car, your food or even your dog. The iPhone 11 also gives you the ability to move the lighting effects of your photo's around using portrait lighting. The iPhone 11 also supports more lighting modes more than the iPhone XR, such as the Stage and Stage Mono.

How to Use the Night Mode Feature

The amount of light entering your camera sensor is measured in the luminance metric (lux) and Apple has designed the Night Mode to work in environments around 10 lux. When you are in a dark environment the luminance metric is about 100 lux, and during twilight or in a poorly lit room the lux value falls between 10-15 lux value. Once the lux value is below 10, the Night Mode will come up automatically, but if the lux value of the environment is not so low, the Night Mode will be suggested if the environment is dark. This would appear at the top left of your iPhone 11 screen in the shape of a crescent moon if you feel the night mode would be necessary, simply tap on the button to toggle it on and it would turn yellow in colour.

Once the Night Mode is enabled you can press down on the shutter button and hold it still for your camera to simulate the long exposure. The camera Night Mode automatically simulates a long exposure from 1 to 3 seconds depending on the lux value of the environment, so if you feel the automatic value it sets for you is not going to give you the best quality, you can always adjust it up to a maximum value of 10 seconds using the slider under the viewfinder.

If you ever feel you don't want the Night Mode when using your camera, you can always toggle off the yellow Nigh Mode button.

How to Take "Slofies" Using Your iPhone 11

With the new iPhone 11 updates, you can now take "slofies" which is a slow-motion video at a frame rate of 120. The word slofie was invented by combining the word slo-mo and the word selfie together. Another feature of the upgraded 12-megapixel front camera is the ability to take a wider shot by flipping the phone landscape, this capability is ideal for group selfies.

To take your slow-motion selfie to follow these steps:

Step 1: Launch your iPhone camera

Step 2: Tap on the perspective flip button under the viewfinder, which is the button on the right side of the big shutter button. This would activate the front camera for you.

Step 3: Next you should select the Slo-Mo option, by swiping through the shooting mode options until the 'Slo-Mo' option is centred on the screen right above the shutter button.

Step 4: Tap on the shutter button to record your slow-motion picture, and when you're done tap on the shutter button once again to end the slofie.

Shooting Videos Fast Using the iPhone 11 QuickTake Feature

You can quickly switch from taking photos into making a video with the improved camera feature. To make videos on previous iPhone versions, you would have to go into the options to select video if you're already in the photo mode.

So you're taking photos and you want to switch from photo mode to video mode on your iPhone 11, simply press down on the shutter button while making your video and let go once you're done to end the recording.

If you want to continue recording without having to hold on to the shutter button, slide the elastic button to the far right and place it on the padlock icon to lock it in place. In this position, you can even take still photos by tapping on the white shutter button. When you are don with your QuickTake tap on the red record button to end it.

Taking Burst Photos with iPhone 11

To take a series of pictures rapidly at 10 frames per second rate, then you should try the burst mode.

Press down the shutter button and drag it to the far left until the elastic shutter is now on the last picture you took. Hold the finger in place, while the camera takes a series of images. You would notice a counter increasing on the original shutter position. This indicates the number of photos taken. Once you're satisfied with the number of photos taken, let go of the shutter button.

With these few tips on how to make the most out of your camera, I would be signing out on this elaborate guide on how to get started with your iPhone 11. I believe I have covered all that you need to enjoy your new iPhone 11. If there are any parts you think I have missed out and would want me to cover, please don't hesitate to drop a message in the review section, I would really love to work with your feedback. Now that you know how powerful your iPhone 11 is, you can wield it with confidence. So, go out there, get creative and don't be afraid to explore other features.